Mercedes
& The Missing Clock

Anuj Khare

Viva Books

New Delhi | Mumbai | Chennai | Kolkata | Bangalore | Hyderabad

Copyright © Viva Books Private Limited
First Published 2007

VIVA BOOKS PRIVATE LIMITED

4737/23, Ansari Road, Daryaganj, New Delhi 110 002
Tel. 42242200, 23258325, 23283121 E-mail: vivadelhi@vivagroupindia.net

Plot No. 76, Service Industries, Shirvane, Sector 1, Nerul, Navi Mumbai 400 706
Tel. 27721273, 27721274 E-mail: vivamumbai@vivagroupindia.net

Jamals Fazal Chambers, 26 Greams Road, Chennai 600 006
Tel. 28294241, 28290304 E-mail: vivachennai@vivagroupindia.net

B-103, Jindal Towers, 21/1A/3 Darga Road, Kolkata 700 017
Tel. 22816713 E-mail: vivakolkata@vivagroupindia.net

7, GF, Sovereign Park Aptts., 56-58, K. R. Road, Basavanagudi, Bangalore 560 004
Tel. 26607409 E-mail: vivabangalore@vivagroupindia.net

101-102, Moghal Marc Apartments, 3-4-637 to 641, Narayanguda, Hyderabad 500 029
Tel. 27564481 E-mail: vivahyderabad@vivagroupindia.net

www.vivagroupindia.com

All rights reserved. No part of this book may be reproduced, stored in a retrieval system, or transmitted in any form or by any means, electronic, mechanical, photocopying, recorded or otherwise, without the written permission of the publishers.

Every possible effort has been made to ensure that the information contained in this book is accurate at the time of going to press, and the publisher and author cannot accept responsibility for any errors or omissions, however caused. No responsibility for loss or damage occasioned to any person acting, or refraining from action, as a result of the material in this publication can be accepted by the editor, the publisher or the author.

ISBN   81-309-0617-1

Published by Vinod Vasishtha for Viva Books Private Limited,
4737/23 Ansari Road, Daryaganj, New Delhi 110 002.

Printed & bound by Sanat Printers, Kundli, Haryana.

CONTENTS

Acknowledgements   vii

Prologue: The Atlantis   1

1. The Turmoil   5
2. The Initiation   12
3. Take Control of Your Life, Now!   17
4. The Philosophy of Time   29
5. Master the Basic Rules   39
6. State Management   61
7. Outcome-Oriented Planning   73
8. Value-Oriented Prioritization   86
9. Time Mastery Techniques   97
10. Beyond Space and Time: Spiritual Approach to Time Mastery   99

Time Mastery Seminar   105

Acknowledgements

Mercedes and the Missing Clock took exactly one year and seventeen days to complete. It is the result of exemplary efforts by some very special people.

Special thanks

- To thousands of readers of *Science of Achievement* and *Psychology of Success in IIT-JEE* who wrote to us via emails and letters to share their success stories.
- To thousands of participants of our Firewalk, Spoon bending, Time mastery and other personal development and empowerment seminars and workshops whose experiences went in as stories in this book.
- To Manya, for being a very special part of my life and supporting me through thick and thin. Also for being the wonderful editor for this book and spending those countless waking nights to get the book released on time.
- To my friends and family, especially Late Shri N. S. Khare, Mrs Anand Kumari Khare, Mr Vijay Khare, Dr Shashi Khare and Rajat Khare.
- To Mr D. P. Sapru and his team at Viva Books for believing in the potential of the book and ensuring excellent production quality.
- To Bhavya Arnav for the fabulous cover.
- To Appin Empowerment team led by Mr Puneet Tiwari and everyone who is a part of Appin Group of companies.

Prologue: The Atlantis

The spaceship landed! The lights were still flashing when the door opened. Three warm bodies walked out of the front door. To an outsider, this would look like a clip from the motion picture *Extra Terrestrial (ET)*. The first sight of the Atlantis was picture-perfect, exactly as I had imagined. It was beyond imagination for Sunny. We put our first steps on the lush green grass of this lost continent. We were rediscovering this magical land. Walking barefoot, we could feel the tenderness of the wet morning grass, cut flawlessly. At a distance, we saw grasslands stretching as far as the eyes could see, the view ending with snow-capped mountains. Monica gazed at some white cows with black spots grazing on our left. As we walked in a mesmerized state exploring this beautiful world, we reached the banks of a river with crystal-clear water. The river must have been about 30 feet deep; still we could see the riverbed loaded with diamond-like objects shining in our eyes. Walking along the riverside, I occasionally glanced at the shoals of fish passing by. They seemed to be looking right at us. I felt they were welcoming our visit to their land. We kept our conversations to a bare minimum. A lot was racing through our minds, but words fall short when you are spellbound. Warm rays of the morning sun along with a cool light breeze and the awesome surroundings were all the conversation we needed. We must have walked for a while when Sunny yelled, "Hey dad, there is a hut behind those trees." We looked in the direction Sunny was pointing but couldn't see anything. The cabin was almost hidden among the trees. "It's right there dad," he shouted pointing in a specific direction.

As we approached the cabin, a healthy-looking couple greeted us. Looking closely, I noted that their skin was glowing like a golden sheet reflecting sunlight. They appeared special. I couldn't help but wonder if this is how we were meant to be had there been no pollution, unhealthy diets and stress. I was amused by the fact that Atlantis was inhabited by humans, just like it is said in the books.

The couple introduced themselves as Joseph and Maria and invited us inside their cosy hut. After the formal introductions during our conversation, we learnt that they had been living in the Atlantis for over 45 years now, and were around 15 when they moved to this magical continent. Both Monica and I exchanged a look because they didn't look a day over 20. Sunny was remarkably friendly with the couple and happily narrated how we had just landed and were going to be here for a while. The warm-hearted couple delightfully heard our experiences so far.

"You know, we are planning to leave for a month-long trip across Atlantis, would you like to join us?" Joseph asked. I looked in Monica's eyes. We wanted to go, but were not sure if we could accept the offer; after all we barely knew Joseph and Maria and it seemed intrusive. We hesitated, but the hospitality of this wonderful couple finally made us agree. We even accepted their invitation to spend the night at their place before we left the next day for the expedition of our life. Sunny couldn't sleep with excitement the whole night.

PROLOGUE: THE ATLANTIS

We woke up in the morning to the first rays of sunshine, but continued to lie on the bed not sure what to do. Maria knocked on the door, "Breakfast's ready." We realized that this would be the first meal we would have after coming here. The previous night, we had gone to bed without dinner in the excitement of the trip. When we stepped out of our room, Joseph was finishing his morning stretching and jogging ritual in the garden. I made a mental note of following a similar routine from the next day, and then recalled the slogan *tomorrow never comes*. I decided to take a walk outside starting today even if it meant for just ten minutes. Honestly, I felt rejuvenated right after the first minute. Sunny was sitting between our hosts, while Monica was sitting next to Maria at the breakfast table when I entered the room. I grabbed the stool next to Maria and was most impressed by the table that had large-sized fresh fruits of all sorts. They had also put freshly-baked bread with some homemade jam, some granola cereal with soy milk; little wonder that Joseph and Maria looked so young; anyone would if they ate such a healthy breakfast.

We started our journey in Joseph's gorgeous yellow sail boat named Aphrodite after the Greek goddess of love. It was 7.30 a.m. by my watch and the day had just begun!

We were sailing down the river with tall tress on either side. Occasionally we could see a deer running across the woods. The smell of freshly cut grass mixed with pine, so unique and heavenly, was almost erotic for me. We stopped by the shore. There were a few people camped along the riverside. This was the first time we had witnessed people other than Joseph and Maria in Atlantis. Everyone was very friendly and made us feel at home. Sunny saw a bunch of kids playing soccer and vanished immediately. Soccer was currently the unconditional love of his life and his excitement reached a climax even at the mere thought of the game in this beautiful countryside.

Monica and Maria decided to put on their bathing suits and go for a dip. The clear water was moderately cool but felt genuinely good in the sun. We watched them for a while when Joseph asked me "Do you want to play golf?" My jaw was left open, "You have golf here, wow! Sure." It was a dream come true. I never had so much time in my life to play golf without worrying about work and checking my watch after every hole. In Atlantis, contrary to my previous experiences with golf, I enjoyed every defining moment of it without the focus ever going on the time. When we returned, Monica and Maria were lying on the beach. I asked Monica if she wished to take another dip, she said yes. I stripped myself to shorts and jumped in the river. We floated for a while and held each other closely. As we got to the middle of the river, I looked in her eyes and noticed her million-dollar smile which had charmed me twelve years ago.

We hadn't been this happy in a long time. Hugging her firmly in my arms, I looked towards the sky. It may have been the first time, but I closed my eyes and said out aloud, "Thank you God, thank you so much." Time stood still. And I wanted the moment to last for ever.

I left Monica and started swimming towards the shore. She wanted to swim for some more time and went a little deeper. Suddenly I heard a scream, and my heart started racing. It sounded like Monica's voice. She screamed again . . .

1

The Turmoil

I turned back instantly, and fell down hard. The bed was about two and a half feet high and it hurt. I woke up from a dream, probably the most beautiful dream I ever had. Monica was still screaming. "John, John, Where are you?" I ran towards the kitchen knowing that's where the voice was coming from. It wasn't difficult anyway given a small one-room apartment. The egg tray had fallen down, and the dozen eggs broke and spilled all over the kitchen floor! Monica was hysterical. I tried to comfort her, but I was frustrated too. This was not the first time such an event had occurred. Something like this happened almost every other day. But I knew it was not Monica's fault; her job was pressing her for time over the month. Our son Sunny was in sixth grade now and needed more attention in his studies. I usually had little time for Sunny. Monica worked full-time as a software trainee from 9 a.m. to 6 p.m. that ran into late nights and even weekends on several occasions. She recently joined the company and wanted to make a positive impression on her manager to make her job permanent.

I asked Monica not to worry about breakfast. I looked in her eyes and said "Honey, I'll make some toast and milk for Sunny while you get ready for work, we can eat on the way to office."

This pacified her a little bit as she kissed me and hurried to grab her clothes and take a shower. She didn't want to be late. I made the toast and poured some chocolate milk for Sunny, who had just woken up. He would be late for school today, I thought. He had not been doing well either in studies or in sports. He was in fact becoming lazier day by day. I decided not to scold him for waking up late as we probably had a lot to contribute to his erratic behaviour. This upset Monica a lot. She stepped out of the shower and Sunny stepped in. In five minutes, she was ready and on her way to work skipping breakfast as usual. She would probably have some coffee and cookies at work. For the first time, I noticed she had put on some weight.

Sunny stepped out of the bathroom, wore his uniform, quickly gobbled his breakfast and left for school. Luckily his school was walking distance now; previously he used to miss his school bus all the time.

I was late for work myself. The situation wasn't great at my office either. Despite working for over 60 hours a week, work always needed more of me. The company was growing at a rapid pace, but I was shrinking even faster. My commitments grew for meeting quarterly targets. Unlike in other organizations, the targets here were manageable. What bothered me was that despite all efforts, a significant portion of the work accumulated for me at the last moment. As a business manager, I was responsible for timely deliveries and because of my poor time management, we screwed up big time in several assignments, which further rippled to my team.

In my early years, I justified my lack of interest towards software development as the cause of poor performance. I had then quit my job as a software engineer, pursued MBA and joined McKinsey & Co as an associate.

My expectations fell flat when the problems transferred to the current job and grew as I slowly grew in designation. I had taken myself with me wherever I went. I knew the issue was time, or actually the lack of it. This lack of proper management of time reflected everywhere in my life. Most of my salary was in the form of bonus which was tied to my performance. The results of course were not up to the mark. This made the finances tight at home. This was the reason both of us had to work despite Sunny needing much attention at this tender age. Monica was not keeping well with her health either. Financial instability had led to problems in our marital life also, although we were trying to handle it maturely.

"Cuckoo, cuckoo," came a loud sound breaking the silence. My attention went to the clock in the main hall; it was 10 a.m. already. I quickly locked the house and drove towards work. I could hear the roars of morning traffic as I tuned the radio to my favourite radio channel, my only source of recreation on most working days. As I put the car in gear I noticed the gas needle indicating a serious dip in fuel. I hurriedly made a left turn towards the main street silently cursing myself under my breath for not refuelling the car the evening before. My thoughts immediately went to the dry-cleaning receipt on the dashboard that Monica had asked me to pick up two days ago. I noticed a brawl on the street between an auto-rickshaw driver and a guy driving a brand new Mercedes. Road rage is a common sight on any big city street and the haste to make it through the day affects every stratum of the society. I felt people including myself often use disagreements anywhere as a means to release pent-up pressures. I made a mental list of my projects for the current month as the radio jockey chirped away about an upcoming book fair. "Must make time to take Sunny for the book fair," I told myself. Monica often cribbed about how we didn't spend enough quality time with our son. I would always defend myself saying I would add the quality for sure if I could make the time first. However, deep down I knew her insinuation was not just for Sunny, but towards our relationship as well. It was amazing the way Monica had turned into a zealous working woman from a carefree laidback person she was before we got married. She worked hard to keep us going as a family, rarely complained about how we didn't spend enough time together anymore doing the things we did which brought us together in the first place.

I was so lost in my thoughts that I crossed my office building. I realized my mistake as I stood before the huge billboard at the intersection, two blocks ahead of my office. The billboard had a new advertisement every Thursday, just like a new movie came out every Friday. Last week this oversized billboard had a picture of a new cherry-flavoured soda launched by Pepsi. Inspired by the billboard, I bought a dozen cans. The advertisement was of a special weekend seminar titled 'Time Mastery'. There was a picture of an ancient broken hour-glass showing sand leaking at the bottom.

That's exactly how I felt; the sands of time were slipping through my fingers and I didn't know how to make change. Before I knew I would be sitting at the dusk of my life with silver streaks in my hair wondering how I could have done things differently. I hadn't even gotten a handle over my life. My first impulse was to jump at the prospect of attending the seminar, but then an afterthought took over.

What was the guarantee the seminar would be able to bring the necessary revolution in my life? What if I end up spending time and money and the situation didn't improve?

I realized I was asking the wrong questions. The question I should be asking is 'What did I have to lose?' Life had already hit rock bottom, what could be worse? Although I never believed that any seminar or workshop could change my life, the current situation suggested I desperately needed a transformation. What I needed was a way to really master time as the billboard implied, but could one really do that? The seminar could only do good for myself and my family. Across-the-board was written in block letters 'Everyone wants to go to heaven, but nobody wants to die.' That was so true, I had been complaining about life, work and time, but was unable to do anything about it except complain. Maybe this seminar was going to open the door to my new life. I called the number listed on the hoarding and booked three tickets with my credit card.

It was Thursday, and the seminar would start from tomorrow. Three days in a countryside location, around 100 kilometres away from where we lived sounded almost like a vacation. There were no seats left; but my persuasion skills had come in handy. I reported sick at the office and took the next three days off. I had been sick for quite a while with all the stress at home and office. I needed to heal myself. Before turning back towards home, I decided to stop by Monica's office. She was bound to crib about the weekend but perhaps that would be a perfect time for us to have a long overdue chat about our lives. She was busy in a meeting, so I waited at the reception. There was a magazine titled *Positive Life* on the coffee table. I picked it up and started browsing. I turned the pages and came across a write-up on the seminar I had just enrolled for. I was instantly more sure of my decision. I felt that this weekend would be the turning point in my life, as well as my family's. Monica came out of her meeting to see me. I expected her to be pleasantly surprised. However, she looked worried as she asked, "Honey, is everything all right?" She had every reason to be shocked that way. After all, I had never paid her a visit during office hours, except for lunch the first week she had joined.

"I took leave from work today. What do you think about this?" I asked, showing her the article on the seminar. She read it patiently and looked at me, without saying a word.

Monica had always been a big believer of learning lessons from experts in life, via books, seminars, audio programmes or whatever channel she came across. I never encouraged her to do so as I always thought that we should learn the lesson of our life ourselves. She would argue that throughout our growing-up years, we learn from our teachers, sports coaches, music instructors and so on, so why is learning a problem when we grow up to be adults? I guess she had a point and I realized it today. Her expression suggested that she knew I finally was beginning to make sense of her ideas, even willing to let my ego aside and take a positive step.

"I am not doing it to please you, I feel the need of a massive change in my life too", I said defensively.

"I would love to go, but how can I take leave at such short notice," said Monica. She was right. I hadn't thought about that at all. I felt foolish in front of her when she learnt that I had already bought the tickets for the three of us.

"Let me try, wait here for a moment," she said as she disappeared back in her office. She came back within 15 minutes looking all excited. "I spoke to my boss, and he is willing to let me off tomorrow if I work next Saturday when he needs me more for a meeting with a client. We are in luck."

It was a fabulous drive to the seminar location. Sunny thought we were going to a retreat for three days, and missing a day from school delighted him. I was thinking how everything came together to make this happen.

We reached the place well before time. I didn't notice it at first, the main speaker at the seminar was named Joseph. Did it have some correlation with the dream I had the previous morning? I wouldn't probably know for sure, but as the seminar started, I knew with certainty that life would never be the same again.

2

The Initiation

I came home from a game of tennis, around 7.30 a.m. Bobby, an associate at the office, was standing at the front door of our house ringing the bell. It surprised me to see him there so early in the morning. He turned around and saw my car pulling up the driveway.

"Congratulations Sir," said Bobby. I looked at him bewildered.

"You don't know? Well . . . " he took a slight pause and then continued, "Sir, you have been promoted to the position of countrywide Chief Executive Officer (CEO) in the company. The news came in late last night, but it seems you haven't heard it as yet."

I was out for dinner with my family and had switched off my mobile phone. Although I was expecting a positive response, the news still came as really a pleasant one and brought a smile to my face. Given that Bobby had a loud voice which grew louder with excitement, it wasn't a surprise that Monica heard him too and she rushed to the driveway. She hugged me and invited Bobby inside the house for breakfast. I guess she wanted to thank him for bringing such wonderful news. Once seated, Bobby couldn't hold his curiosity that was clear from his face the moment I saw him in the driveway. He blurted, in awe, "Two promotions in three years – from 'Senior Business Manager' to 'Vice President, Marketing', to CEO. New house, new car and perfect health. To top that a pleasure trip every month and an international vacation every year. Jesse even mentioned that your son Sunny is doing great in school, thanks to the time you spend with him. Is there a secret to this transformation?"

"Relax Bobby," I said taking a deep breath. "You haven't taken a moment between all those statements."

I thought about it, maybe it was a big deal for most people. At one time, it was a huge deal for me, I would never have believed it was possible for anyone, let alone myself.

But it was true, wasn't it? Coming from Bobby I realized that perhaps it was a truly amazing situation.

I wanted to answer Bobby's question. Besides being a colleague at work, he was also an old friend. Although he was about five years junior to me, we spent some time together being on the football team for almost a year back in school. But I still wasn't sure if I could explain it to him. I shrugged the topic off with a joke.

"Do you know the most confused race in the world, Bobby?" I asked.

Bobby was startled at the question. He thought for a while and replied in the negative.

"It's the Egyptians," I answered.

"What?" he asked confused at my answer.

"Because their daddy becomes a mummy after dying." And we both laughed out loud.

I excused myself to get ready for work while Bobby chatted with Monica.

I decided to give Bobby a ride to work. As I opened the garage door and stepped in the car, I waited for Bobby to get in from the other side. I saw Bobby staring at the car with adoration in his eyes. He sighed, "A silver S-class Mercedes. What I wouldn't do to have one of these."

"Well, hop in," I said. Once seated, Bobby seemed to really enjoy the interiors of the car. He was so awestruck that he even forgot he had been meaning to speak with me about something important.

I noticed he was staring at the dashboard. "You don't have a clock in the car! Did you get it removed?" Bobby asked. His focus, for some reason, also went to my wrist. "You are not wearing a watch either! How do you keep track of time?"

Bobby had asked a million dollar question. I replied, "There is a prevalent belief that one has to work round the clock, always keep track of time and manage it every second for being successful in life. I on the other hand followed a ritual of *timelessness*, rather than rigorous time management."

Bobby partially understood what I had said. He seemed to be solving the mystery of Mercedes and the missing clock!

We reached office and parked in the basement. Bobby dropped in at my new office cabin during lunch. He had the same question. "How do you manage it?" I again changed the topic by assigning him some urgent work. Not that I didn't want to share my secret; I wasn't sure if he was ready for it.

The office organized a small party that evening to celebrate my promotion as the CEO. It was 11 p.m. by the time I reached home.

Monica looked over the dashboard a little tensed as she noticed a familiar figure outside the garage door. As the car drew closer I could see Bobby pacing on our front porch. As I pulled into the driveway, Bobby frantically reached for the car door.

"Bobby, is everything all right?" I asked.

"Yeah . . . I mean *no*, John. Everything is not all right," he replied.

I could sense the tension in his voice as he fidgeted with his cell phone and wiped the beads of sweat from his forehead.

"Well, why don't you come in, and we'll talk" I said.

"Thanks John, I mean I'm sorry to bother you so late, no really I mean it. I know you've just come back from a celebration, but I had to talk to you. I don't even know how to begin, but I realize I need to do it. My life's all messed up. Nothing is the way it should be. Even Rita's threatened to leave if things don't get better. I don't know who else to talk to. You have to help me John, please."

"Bobby, Bobby, relax. You're obviously very stressed out. It's almost midnight. Does Rita know you're here?" I asked.

"No," he replied.

"Well, then I suggest you go home, take a hot shower and get some sleep. I promise we'll talk soon. Everything will be fine." As I reassured Bobby, Monica brought out tall glasses of iced lemonade.

Bobby muttered an "I-guess-you're-right" under his breath, gripped the drink and slowly made his way for the door.

The outburst didn't solve his problem but surely gave him some respite.

I remembered a time not too long ago when I went through a similar phase. I realized now that time indeed was in your own hands.

The next day was quite busy, and I didn't get to see Bobby at all. I left early morning for a seven-day training programme at a hill resort out of the city. On the plane as I sat and sipped my iced tea, my thoughts wandered to Bobby's situation. I realized that I needed to collect my views before I met him the next day.

All the training programmes were quite similar, which included various lectures and discussions about how we could first increase and then sustain our market share. The last lecture ended at 6.20 p.m. when we decided to call it a day.

The resort was beautiful particularly in the evening. I invited Bobby to my cottage as I barely had a chance to talk to him after the incident outside my home. I knew he had several questions for me. It was obvious from the way he glanced at me several times throughout the day. After all, I had promised to talk to him the next day, and it had been a couple of days now.

Bobby reached at 8 p.m. sharp. His eyes told me that he had a lot of expectations. I was prepared . . .

3

Take Control of Your Life, Now!

I had a conference call and ordered room service instead of going to the buffet. I had just finished dinner when Bobby arrived. I asked him if he had eaten. "Yes, just a few minutes ago," he said. "So what is in your mind?" I asked.

Bobby had a hopeful expression in his eyes when he came in. But the blunt question threw him off guard. He looked at me with a solemn look in his face and whispered, "Don't you know?"

"I guess I do, but would still like to hear it from you," I replied.

Bobby sighed and began, "I will be honest. What I would really like is to become a master of time like you. I want all the simple things in life personally and professionally. Just like everyone else I want happiness. I don't know if it's too much to ask for, but I am in a state where I desperately need to ask you what is the key to really solve the mystery of time. I have this belief that you are the only one who can help me. I thought you would do this for our years of friendship. Wouldn't you? I promise to implement everything you say."

"Sure buddy," I said instantaneously, relieving the rising pressure in the room created by Bobby's emotional outburst. I did want to inquire from him though, on how all of a sudden he developed this sudden strong instinct of learning time mastery. His actions were speaking volumes about his determination to learn it, or else I would not have invited him to my room. It was important for me to understand if he would have the determination to implement what it took because one of the principles of time mastery is to invest time wisely.

Many people want to learn 'time mastery', but when they see that practising this art needs substantial commitments, especially in the beginning, they back off. I know that it is as foolish as saying that one doesn't have enough time to stop for fuelling your car, but many people think exactly like that. A few reasons why people think they should manage time are: time is in fact the greatest resource, it is irreversible; one could contribute more if they had more time; mastering time would make one work smarter not harder, which is the key to success; it is a source of energy, positivity and higher self-esteem. But these reasons are not enough in today's world to motivate a person to practise time mastery.

Before I could speak, Bobby blurted "I know that you want to ensure that I want to practise time mastery. I understand you value your time."

He seemed to read my mind; I didn't bother to ask how. He continued, "My life is transparent to you. I have hit the absolute rock bottom in life, failing in almost all areas. I don't have either the time or energy to do anything. My wife and kids are always complaining about my making promises and breaking them. My health is a mess. I have constant headaches and backaches. I haven't had a promotion for almost two years, and there is no chance of getting one in the near future. Most importantly, I hardly get any time for myself. I had lost all hope until I saw the transformation in you. The massive change you brought in your life opened my mind to what all is possible.

I, for the first time in my life, believe there is hope, and I believe you have the key.

"The key lies within you, Bobby," I quickly remarked with a smile.

I knew that he was ready for the initiation. His eyes told me; he had a good enough reason. It is a known fact that unless one has a strong reason, one cannot bring any form of change in life. He was determined to learn, understand, implement and practise 'time mastery'.

I was thinking out aloud. Many people think that managing time is too cold and lacks spontaneity. They even go the extent of saying that they love being late and messy, and the people who manage time are boring and lead dull lives.

This is only a myth though; would one have more spontaneity in life when one has enough time or when they were constantly running from one chore to another hardly having any time at all. I understand that many people take 'time mastery' to an extreme form and become sticklers for time management. I am not talking about those kind of people either. Once one gets over these negative beliefs and builds a positive determination to be a master of their time, 'time mastery' is an easy task.

I guess I must have been thinking for a while because when I came back to my worldly senses, I found Bobby staring at me. It was time now to start.

"What do you understand about 'time mastery'?" I inquired.

Bobby instantly replied, "It's about doing more in less time." He paused and continued, "That's what the book said."

Why was I expecting that answer? The answer Bobby gave is what everyone believes 'time mastery' is all about. However, there happens to be a fine distinction between the words 'time mastery' and 'time management'.

Most of the self-help books and seminars focus on 'time management'. There is nothing wrong with 'time management'. On the contrary, it is an important part of the time mastery process. The problem comes when we treat 'time management' as the only important aspect of 'time'. In reality, it ranks quite low among the several elements one needs to master to experience true joy in life.

"Bobby, before we go further, let me shed light on what I can offer. I don't teach 'time management'. In case you wish to learn how to do more in less time, you would need to go elsewhere", I said.

Bobby was puzzled. I went in depth to explain to him what I meant before I scared him off.

"See, doing a few more tasks in a day will not necessarily give happiness and satisfaction to an individual. On the other hand, doing so does have the potential of making someone even more overwhelmed. *Time mastery, if rightly understood, is a vision to improve the quality of life by creating more time in life for what really matters.* In essence 'time mastery' is all about understanding what really matters to one in life and how one creates time for the same, for this is what would bring the ultimate level of joy and fulfilment in one's life. Understanding and implementing this very principle is exactly what transformed my life."

This seemingly new idea of 'time mastery' did have an effect on Bobby, as he realized that he was focusing his energy in the wrong direction and therefore not getting the desired results.

Despite the revelation he was still not totally convinced. He asked, "John, is it possible for me to take out time for what I really like? Theoretically, it sounds excellent, but can it become a reality?"

I answered his question with a counter question "Bobby, have you heard the story of the wise man of Samparan?"

"No," Bobby replied.

I continued with the story:

> Once there was a wise man who lived in Samparan. Everyone in the village came to him for counselling. In the same town, there also lived two boys who devised a scheme to make a fool of the wise man. They planned to capture a baby sparrow and as one of the boys cupped the bird in his hands, the other would ask the wise man to guess what the first boy was holding. As a set-up, the boy would let a few tail feathers show between his fingers. The wise man being the wise one would surely announce with pride that it was a baby sparrow, the boys would then ask if it was alive or dead. If the wise man said 'dead', the boy will release the bird which will fly away immediately. And if he said that it was 'alive', the boy would crush the bird in his hands and let it fall to the ground. Thus, independent of what the wise man would answer, the boys would make a fool of him. So, with the baby sparrow cupped securely in his hands, the boy and his friend confronted the wise man and said, "Oh, wise one, what do I have in my hands?" Seeing a few tail feathers showing between the boy's fingers, the wise man declared, "You are holding a baby sparrow." The wise man's quick response told the boy that his scheme was working, so the boy inquired, "Is it alive or dead?" The old man thought for a while, and replied, "It is in your hands."

It is in your hands.

Bobby got his answer. The success of our sessions and books in improving the quality of his life depended on him. The amount of benefit he could derive from my teachings was in his hands. It is possible for him to wake up at six in the morning and be excited about life. It is possible to have the perfect relationship with his wife, parents and kids. It is possible to have the desired financial freedom. It is also possible to be in a state of joy all the time. It only lies in his hands. He had no one else but himself to blame for the poor quality of life and only himself to thank for the positive transformation he was about to bring in his life.

Bobby pitched in, "John, I understand that improving the condition of my life is in my hands, and what I do with it is also in my control." He paused for a moment and then continued. "But if everything is in my hands, does it mean that I can control the traffic and weather also?"

That was a funny question Bobby asked. I answered, "No you can't, Bobby. Even though we can't control unpredictable things like the weather or the traffic, we can control what we make out of the situation. If we meet traffic on the way back home, we can either curse it or we can choose to accept it. We can choose to make the best use of the time by listening to life-enhancing audio books or music or try to find alternative ways to avoid the situation. In case it is raining outside when we have an urgent task to finish, we can either complain about the situation or choose to stay at home and try and accomplish whatever we can being indoors. We can watch the rain with a cup of herbal tea, or the young at heart may even run out and play with the kids in the rain.

"Always remember the law of nature, we can never change the events, but how we interpret them is completely in our hands. You may have heard of this prayer before – *God, give me the serenity to have the courage to change what I can change, to graciously accept what I cannot change and have the wisdom to understand the difference between the two.* Bobby, the gist of whole time mastery or even life mastery is hidden in these few lines."

Bobby interrupted my speech pointing his finger at the window. I turned back and saw streaks of flashing light outside. We went outside to have a closer look. There were a few glowworms moving between the trees appearing as miniature flashlights moving at a rapid pace. The view was magical, something you may never see in cities. We watched the worms in fascination for some time and then decided to walk to the café in the resort. It looked like it would rain soon.

It started raining as we reached the café. We sat down and ordered a cup of tea each as we continued with our conversation. "Well Bobby, tell me honestly, where do you think you stand in your life right now?" I asked.

"Not at a nice place, I guess," answered Bobby. "In fact it's as low as it gets."

As sadistic it may sound, I was pleased to hear his answer. "Great, at least you are willing to admit it. One of the fundamentals in making 'time mastery' principles work in life is to accept reality as it is. Most people use softeners in life. Statements like 'It's not so bad', 'I am not that fat' and so on make people resistant to change. I am not saying that one should be critical of everything in life, but mostly, the use of such softeners limits one's ability to improve the quality of their life. First, we need to see our life as it is. It is important to be able to understand the three basic steps in progress: quantify where we stand today, understand the direction in which we wish to proceed and quantify our progress in a timely fashion."

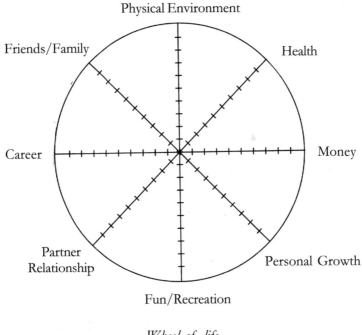

Wheel of life

It started pouring heavily by now. We realized that we may be here for some time. They were playing Mozart in the café; the music had a soothing effect. I asked for a pencil and pad from the waiter.

I drew a large circle with the pencil. Then I gave eight different labels at equal intervals on the rim of the circle and connected them with the centre. Bobby was curious about the whole exercise. I broke the suspense, "Bobby, we call it a wheel of life. And the eight areas of life, namely money, personal growth, fun and recreation, partner relationship, career, friends and family, physical environment and health are it's spokes that give it the structure. The centre of the wheel represents 'zero', a state of total collapse in levels of joy and fulfilment in that specific area. The points at the circumference of the circle represent a 'ten', a state of absolute bliss and contentment. Let us see where you stand in your life right now in all these areas."

Bobby stared at me for a while. I looked at him too. Finally he broke the silence, "Do you mean that you actually want me to do it? You mean I should consciously think where I stand in life right now and quantify it with numbers from zero to 10?"

"Yes Bobby, I actually want you to do it. Unless you are clear about where you stand, what are we going to work on? Remember, 'time mastery' is less about learning and more about execution. We won't go any further until you finish the exercise. Go ahead and fill it right here, even if it takes the whole night."

Bobby took my advice very seriously. Sometimes one has to be persuasive to get the job done, especially when you are passionate about the cause. I looked at Bobby with amusement. He was trying to quantify his present and was engrossed in his thought, trying to dig into his soul. I understood that it was a hard task and would take time; how often do we stop and think where exactly we stand in life. I took a break and sat down on the covered patio in a meditative pose and closed my eyes. I focused my attention on the falling water droplets and slowly entered the state of completeness and total peace and relaxation. I had come to realize that in certain meditative states, one hour of relaxation equals two hours or more of sleep. Using these techniques, I cut short my sleeping time to four–six hours from the eight–ten hours a day I normally used to sleep earlier. There was absolutely no compromise on energy; in fact I felt more energetic now. Initially, it was a little hard to break the years of sleep conditioning, but with time the new habit slowly but steadily set in. In about five minutes of meditative time, all my thoughts subsided and I entered a state of thoughtlessness. Even if a thought came by, I replaced it with the thought of eternal breath.

I don't know how long I must have been in this state; all I remember is a lightning that threw me out of state. When I walked back into the room, awakened and refreshed, Bobby was finishing his wheel.

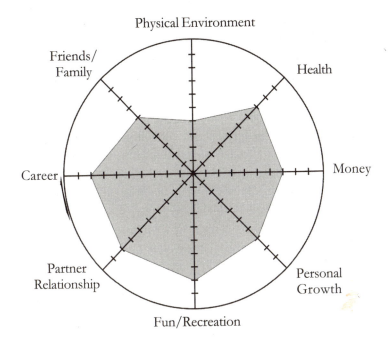

Wheel of life (actual)

He looked up to see me without realizing that I was away for a while. I looked at the paper and saw all the ratings he had given to each area and points he had marked on the straight line joining the centre to the rim showing his rating graphically.

I then asked him to join all the consecutive points, forming his wheel of life, which was far from being the circle that represents a balanced life. "Bobby, if this was the wheel of your car called life, how would the journey be?" I asked Bobby.

Bobby looked at his wheel and started murmuring. "I had no idea how unbalanced my life was. No wonder I was having a rough ride. Honestly, my butt hurts just looking at this wheel."

I smiled and then pitched in, "Bobby, through time mastery, we aim to smoothen this wheel and then preserve the circular alignment while growing its size to receive continuous growth and fulfilment in life."

The clock struck 1 a.m. I had to get up early to prepare for the next day's meeting. Bobby wasn't sure if he was ready to sleep yet. "John, I want to sleep now so I feel refreshed in morning, but I just don't feel like sleeping for some reason. What do I do?"

I had a one-liner ready for Bobby. "Fake it until you make it."

This mantra applies everywhere in life. In case you feel depressed, fake a smile and after a while you would actually start smiling. In case you can't sleep, fake it as if you were sleepy and after a little while you would fall off to sleep.

The rain had stopped by now. We walked back to my cottage. On the way I advised him to repeat the following line: "I am enjoying learning about time mastery."

I wanted to give him a thought to ponder as he put himself to sleep today. "Act or pretend as if you are the master of your time. How would you act? What would you do? How would you think?"

4

The Philosophy of Time

The meeting ended at 4.25 p.m. I was in the mood for playing tennis. I asked Bobby if he would like to join me. He agreed wholeheartedly. We used to play some tennis during high school. It would be several years now, or should I say decades, since we played against each other. I went back to my cottage and quickly dressed for the game.

I loved playing several sports, and tennis was one of my favourites besides football. The best part about sports, apart from being good for health, is the total involvement one has for the game. Hundred per cent involvement in an activity at both mental and physical level is an absolute must in any sport.

Bobby was already practising on the wall when I reached the courts. The resort courts were well lit, and were right next to the swimming pool. I looked at the lazy chairs by the poolside and decided where we would have today's time mastery sessions after the game.

The game was very refreshing. Bobby was definitely a better player. But with my energy and regular practice I put up quite a fight before John's superb ball control. We decided to take a quick shower followed by a dip in the pool.

I stepped out of the pool and swiftly made my way towards Bobby who was sitting on a lazy chair sipping iced tea. I gestured to a passing waiter to get the same drink for me. I settled in and turned towards Bobby. "What is time?" I asked matter-of-factly. He looked at me like I had put him on the spot. Of late everything I said seemed to have a deeper meaning for him.

"I don't have a watch by me," he replied, simply.

I smiled. "Bobby, I am not asking you for the time, the question I am asking is, 'what exactly is time?' In other words, how do you define time?"

"What is time? Well. I am not sure, yet," he replied sleepily. "Time is an entity that measures . . . hmm . . . time, I guess," he continued.

What is time?

Watching him struggle for a reply, I came to the rescue. "Many people say time is powerful, time is almighty or time is something that runs life and so on. These statements represent characteristics of time, but none of them really defines time. For all practical purposes, without going into a truly scientific definition, *time is an entity that a clock measures.* Assuming that all clocks in the world, be it digital or hourglass or any other kind, measure more or less the same value, the definition of time is universal around the world."

I continued "Understanding this new outlook on 'time' is an initiation to the wisdom of 'time mastery'. Once we understand that time is nothing more than what a clock measures, we can change how we look at this physical entity.

"See Bobby, our forefathers invented 'time' to serve humans, to help them improve the quality of their lives. But we didn't realize when it took over and started controlling us. A simple shift in psychology on how we look at the entity can bring a massive shift in the quality of our lives and make us masters of time," I explained.

Bobby looked puzzled. I continued, "See, all answers come through questions. I am going to ask you another question. What is a map?"

"Well, I can answer that one," chuckled Bobby. "A map is a representation of an actual territory."

"That's right. A map is in fact merely a representation of a territory and not the territory itself. They are not to be confused as being the same. Let us take another example. For many years you may have taken the most suitable route from your house to work. I'm sure you made a mental map after careful study of all the alternatives available. Now, unless an obstruction of some kind namely a new flyover or some unforeseen construction comes up, you continue the tried and tested route indefinitely. This change, however may force you to create a new mental map and find an alternative course, the next most feasible one.

A map cannot represent a territory in totality. There are several features in an actual territory which may not be illustrated on a map.

Understanding the difference between map and territory was pivotal in understanding 'time'. I decided to dig further to drive the point home. I looked at Bobby and said, "Imagine that you are hiking in the Himalayas in Nepal and your goal is to travel from Kathmandu to the Mount Everest base camp with the help of a hiking map. You reach a point where the map says that you go straight from where you are standing, but there is actually a lake in front, would you still walk ahead?"

"Of course not," said Bobby. "I will most probably start walking on the side and try to resume the path on the other side of the lane".

I had made my point. Anyone in the given situation would know that the map is mere a guide to assist you in your journey. But human experience and personal judgment are far more reliable than any map.

Time is a mere representation of an actual experience we have in life, not the experience itself. If the 'time map' is not serving us, maybe it is time to change it. The goal of 'time' is to assist us in our journey of life, just like the map. It is an illustration of a dimension or an aspect of life. We should use it as a guideline only, to assist us in working together in a dynamic environment. We should not let it govern our life but choose to use it for improving the quality of our life. The experiences and emotions one goes through in life are far more important than any time measurement.

Many people complain about their 'weight'. You often hear "I hate myself for being overweight." It is **true** that everyone wants to be in shape, look good and feel good, and weight is a measurement of all these. But is weight the only criterion? Is the goal to lose weight, be fit, healthy and vibrant without paying consideration to weight?

"Is the chair taken?" Both Bobby and I turned to see a svelte lady standing behind us. "No," I said politely. I could see the admiration in Bobby's eyes. The lady must be in her mid-thirties but had obviously been taking excellent care of herself. I turned Bobby's attention away from her and said "In the first seminar I attended on time mastery, a certain participant named Suzanne shared her story. Suzanne was really keen on losing weight but she had not reduced a single kilo. After a lot of thinking she realized that the reason she failed at the weight was because she just wasn't motivated enough to do so. She had been an expert swimmer growing up. However, she had completely stayed away from the pool as she felt that she was too big for the bathing suit.

"She struggled for months to loose a target weight of ten kilograms and failed. Until one day while sorting some old clothes from her college days she came across her old red and white bathing suit. She looked at it for a few minutes and came up with a new target. This time, instead of chasing a number on the weighing machine she would work at herself to fit into her favourite bathing suit. Five weeks, a changed diet plan and fifteen hours of aerobics later, Suzanne hadn't lost her exact ten kilos but fitted into the bathing suit perfectly. Mission accomplished! Thus, by bringing a simple shift in her psychology that weight was just a measurement to assist her in life and not to perpetually put her down, she was able to achieve her real goal of being fit and healthy.

"The philosophy of time mastery follows a similar principle. To be a master of time, you have to start treating time as a measurement, nothing more, nothing less. In the seminar, we did a specific meditation, where each participant was asked how much time they thought they had spent in the meditative state. And each participant had a different answer ranging from five to thirty minutes, whereas the actual clock time spent was over an hour. This clearly indicates that clock time is incapable of capturing our experience which is the core driving force in life.

"Bobby, have you ever been in such a place in nature, where you were sitting on the grass, watching the sunrise and reflecting upon how perfect your life was and never realized that the whole day had passed by? You may even have felt that it was one of the most productive days of your life."

Bobby looked startled. "I often go to the company's resort by the riverside to brainstorm on projects at work. I generally sit on the beach and often lose track of time while I get a lot of ideas. Surprisingly, many a time I don't even feel hungry all day."

Bobby continued, "I get what you are saying about time being a measurement; it could probably never measure my experience when I am on the beach with just myself."

I was happy that Bobby started to understand the philosophy of time and time mastery. To make it clearer, I continued to explain further. "Bobby, I am sure that like everyone else, you too would have been in circumstances where you waited for someone, or attended a boring meeting and five minutes seemed like five hours."

The expression on Bobby's face confirmed that his answer to this question was a 'yes'. "Now how do you explain 'time', when a five-hour activity can seem like a five-minute one and a five-minute activity can seem like five hours? This is an important question and understanding time needs us to explore the answer to this question. A clock would measure both the 'times' similarly, but do we feel that both 'times' are actually the same? What is more important, the clock time or the perceived time? There is no right or wrong answer to this question; we have to choose and define our own reality."

"I understand what you are saying. But would a simple shift in this psychology take my awareness of time to the next level?"

"Absolutely. See, any transformation has to first be conceived in the mind. You used to start looking at time as a measurement only. You can choose to become its master as opposed to having it run your life. This simple step will lead to a massive transformation. This shift in paradigm, with other principles we will discuss later, will bring the changes you want to see in yourself and your environment."

The biggest pitfall one needs to avoid is thinking that time is linear. Let us say that you have an activity that needs four days to complete. You take three days to accomplish half the task. Is it possible to finish the rest of the work in the stipulated time? In case your answer is 'no', you believe in the linear concept of time. I myself was a big believer in the linearity of time until I attended Dr Barbara's software engineering class at the University of Texas, Austin, where I was pursuing a master's degree. One day, Dr Barbara brought an empty jar to the class. She took out some big stones from her blue jute bag and started putting them in the jar one by one. When she couldn't fit in any more stones, she asked us if the jar was full. We said yes; she obviously couldn't put in any more stones. Next she took out pebbles from her bag and filled in the spaces between the stones. She looked at us and asked the same question: "Is the jar full?" We were prepared this time. We knew there was still some space left. Knowing that our response would be a 'no' this time, she took out some sand from another bag and started filling the jar till she couldn't fill any more. The jar was obviously full now. There was no visible space left. Guessing what her next question would be, I stood up and without waiting for her to speak, I said "Dr Barbara, the jar is full now." She looked at the class and asked if they all agreed with me. A few students said yes, and a few no. While listening to the response, she took a sip of water and then started to pour the water slowly in the jar. The sand absorbed all the water.

We had learnt our lesson. There was always some space left in the jar whenever we thought it was full. Dr Barbara explained, "Don't start believing that a project will take a certain

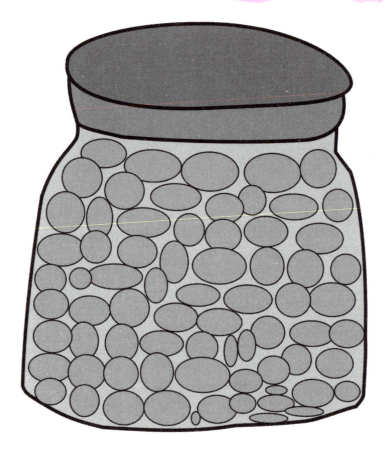

Is the jar full?

fixed time. You could always do it in less and less time, just like the jar can take more and more stuff."

Sheila, our porject group leader, was perhaps the most inquisitive of the lot. She got up and said "I'm sure there is more to this lesson, Dr Barbara. Are you going to tell us there is still space left in the jar?" Dr Barbara smiled and took out paper sachets of salt and sugar from her bag. She poured them in the water and they were absorbed instantly. We clapped. She finished the experiment saying, "I don't have a refrigerator here, else we could freeze the water in the jar and could create some more space."

I knew in my heart that I had just learnt one of the most important lessons in my life. We currently consider distance as linear, but supersonic jets will shake the notion of 'distance linearity' soon. It is only a matter of time till we have teleportation devices that will break the myth of linearity in distances.

It was late in the evening. We decided to walk back to our rooms. It was unusually dark for some reason and we walked slowly. Bobby commented, "We should have carried flashlights and we would have reached our rooms faster and saved time. John, do you believe the accessibility to gizmos and gadgets can save us a lot of time?"

His statement reminded of the excerpt I had read from *The Household Economy* by Scott Burns. Scott says, "We need time. We need time to work, to eat, to sleep, and to accomplish all the daily chores of living. We also need time to know and understand our mates, our children, and our friends. Most of our relationships, in fact, require more time than we have, and it is difficult to avoid the feeling that we could never have enough. Nor is our list of demands on our time complete. We have ignored the time we need to be alone, a necessary but invariably short-changed period. All these demands come before the proliferating hardware used to consume still more time – before the possession, use, and maintenance of necessary equipment such as automobiles, small and large boats, tennis rackets, skis, and golf clubs, sewing machines and looms, bathing suits, hi-fi sets, tape decks and cameras. All these items – the inevitable trappings of affluence – make still more demands on our ever-diminishing store of time. They are responsible for many of the sour notes sounding as affluence and become more general and more disappointing . . .

Economist Staffan Burenstam Linder explores these limits. If it requires time to produce things, it also requires time to maintain and consume them. While this may seem obvious to the harried, we neglect this in most economic literature. Let us assume that each worker has sixteen hours to 'spend' and each hour of productive work requires a half hour of maintenance or time for personal work such as eating, dressing and washing; the worker also requires a half hour of consumption time. Then we can expect an increasing pressure on our available time if we produce an increasing amount of goods in our hours of directly productive work. If a new machine doubles the output of goodies, we then will have twice as much product for the same amount of work. While this may be a delight, it also means that we have twice as much consuming and maintenance to do in our 'nonworking' hours. Thus we become even more harried as our productivity increases."

Dr Scott drove the final point home. I simplified it for Bobby. "In essence, no amount of material goods or industrialization or gadgets like PDAs or robots would simplify our lives. The only way to simplify life is to rely on our conscience and make the right choices. Life will be a lot easier if we mastered a few basic rules."

I wished him good night as we approached the cottage . . .

5

Master the Basic Rules

"John, I think I have started to get a hang of it now. To be honest with you, I didn't expect to get such clarity on things I was too afraid to even confront all this time, but I can feel it in my gut that the transformation may just be what is needed to change things for me. Time and the ability to master it is sure underrated, is there more?

Bobby's comment amused me, but I didn't react.

It had been a couple of days since our last discussion on 'time mastery'. It was crisp, slightly sunny afternoon and the front lawns seemed a good place to enjoy the good weather. The meeting had ended before lunch, and we had a lot more time to ourselves. Scott, our Vice President – Operations, led the session and ended it on a humorous note. He said, "A bus station is where a bus stops, a train station is where a train stops, on my desk I have a workstation . . ."

Bobby needed to understand that unlike the bus or train, learning never stops. "Bobby, we need to understand that time mastery is a cultivated habit and a lifelong learning process; not something you study, pass an exam and get done with. Building the psychology is important, along with mastering the mechanics."

As I tried to explain this to Bobby, he was resistant as he did not initially understand that it had to be woven into his lifestyle. Obviously, he was thinking about it as a one-time lesson that he could learn and that would spell an answer to all his problems. I had a perfect anecdote for this one. I asked Bobby, "Do you brush your teeth every morning?"

"Of course I do," he replied immediately.

I continued, "Why don't you do it once and forget about it? Why every day? Well, let me help you out here," I answered myself. When you're small, you are taught to brush your teeth every day so over a period of time you condition yourself to form a habit. Now, brushing your teeth is part of your routine. The idea of time mastery works the same way. To begin with, one must understand that once this idea settles in your life as a routine feature, like brushing the teeth, eating food, or exercise it will manifest itself in you."

"Absolutely sir," exclaimed Bobby, as he rose and gestured a mock salute in my direction.

I felt an inner satisfaction that Bobby was making progress in understanding the idea. An open mind and an initial will to change are perhaps the only prerequisites of a transformation, but we still had a long way to go. I started to unravel the second layer of the learning essentials for time mastery. And this layer comprised some basic rules that one needs to embed in one's subconscious mind. These rules when followed have the power to improve the quality of an individual's life immediately.

"Bobby, let's get down to the basic principles of mastery now. I guarantee that if you follow these principles religiously, you will make progress in your life."

And Bobby listened patiently, for hours together . . .

MASTER THE BASIC RULES

Rule 1: Make best use of your time now

Because time is a limited resource apportioned to us at birth, an essential step necessary in managing time is deciding which specific activity we should be doing at any given moment. This will serve as a starting point for a more deliberate and controlled use of time in the future. A simple solution for all who feel that they are unable to decide which activities to undertake in their limited time, it is best to ask: *'What is the best use of my time, now?'* The first answer that comes to your mind will be the right answer.

There was a woman named Tina, who attended the time mastery seminar with her family. We discussed the *'Best use of time, now'* principle in one of the sessions. The following day, all the candidates were asked if they were able to apply any lesson they learnt the day before. Tina had an incident to share. Their family sat down in their room after the session when her dad switched on the television. Their family was delighted to see their favourite movie playing on a popular channel. After sometime, Tina's mind asked, 'what is the best use of my time now?' She immediately got the answer that she needed to sleep so she could get up early the next day and do some yoga. This would ensure that she remains energetic throughout the day at the seminar to get the most out of it. And that is exactly what she did. She went to bed and woke up early the next morning, did yoga, and was one of the most energetic people in the seminar.

There could be several ways to classify your activities and judge their usefulness. But the best way is to ask, 'what is best use of my time now?' I would dub it the WBTN principle. Whenever you are unsure about what is the end use of what you are doing, especially when you are doing activities such as aimlessly browsing the net, walking around the corner of your block daydreaming, trying to focus your wandering mind on some work, or merely playing with your cell phone and calling up your friends one by one, *stop immediately*. Without fooling anyone, least of all your own self, ask yourself a serious question, 'What is the best use of my time now?'

Remember, the first answer that comes to the mind while using the 'What is the Best use of my Time Now' principle would be an opinion which has the maximum impact on your future. Activities including spending time with the family, taking up an extra credit course for knowledge enhancement, doing a project that will bring a promotion and an increased salary could all be dubbed as high-impact activities. Entertainment, especially attending a concert that will become a part of your lifetime memory, would also be a high-impact activity. And, by this token, activities such as going out for lunch every day, browsing the internet or watching mindless television would be called low-impact activities. It doesn't mean that we should not do these activities; it only means that it is important to keep a tab on such activities.

The WBTN principle can in fact apply to any situation, especially when you are indecisive. The light of this principle is in its simplicity. As smart people we are taught to ponder and probe over almost every action we take in life. However, we fail to realize that our conscious analysis of every situation may be clouded by various things, such preconceived notions, fears, inhibitions, stress, influence, etc. All of these can often result in us doing things which are perhaps not the best use of our time. The WBTN principle urges you to look within yourself and listen to your inner instincts. Our subconscious mind is a powerhouse of information and works in an extremly scientific manner. It analyses any situation in a multidimensional fashion and is programmed to give us the most feasible option possible if only we listen to it.

So whenever you are unsure about your decision about time and its optimum use, listen to your inner voice. Independent of the situation, it will give you the right answer whenever you need it, without the need for the detailed analysis we just did.

Rule 2: Don't say Yes when you want to say No

Tell me if this sounds familiar: you agreed to do something for someone even though you didn't have time for it. It might be an unreasonable request from a friend, a neighbour, a close relative, a family member or colleague at work. Your boss may ask you to work late when you already had a dinner appointment. You often agree because you feel the other person would feel bad if you said 'no'. It is hard to say 'no' as you feel you will let the other person down if you say 'no'. You feel *guilty* even before you respond! So you say 'sure', even though doing so is going to put you under tremendous stress and pressure. You know you will probably end up resenting it because your heart is just not in it, but you go ahead and agree anyway.

Why are we so afraid to say 'no' to people? For some reason, we were taught that 'no' is disrespectful and sometimes even insulting. We value other people's time more than our own, feeling that we need to bend over backwards to accommodate others, even if it inconveniences us. I know this may have started to sound selfish, but let's be reasonable! 'No' is actually one of the healthiest words that can come out of your mouth. When you say 'no', to someone, you are really saying that you understand and accept your own limitations, and don't want to do a bad job by overwhelming yourself. You are saying that you value your time and priorities and are not willing to sacrifice the truly important things in your life. Respecting one's space and time is not being selfish but valuing one's own identity.

Yes or No?

For example, an acquaintance of yours asks you out for a movie on a Monday night even though you have agreed to go shopping with one of your friends and would therefore stay home and study tonight. You want to say no, but you hate turning people down. Apply the WBTN principle and you'd get the same answer.

Saying 'no' makes time for things that are most important. It is also important for your internal value system, self-esteem and self-confidence. By doing contrary to what you believe in, you are letting yourself down in front of your own eyes. A habit of saying 'yes' when you want to say 'no' may have much more dire consequences and affect your life much deeper than you know. Always saying 'yes' when you want to say 'no' can make you fall in a trap where you may perpetually have to do things you don't want to.

Let me share the experience of Mr Truman from the seventeenth century. One day Mr Truman came out of his hut and saw a banana peel lying in front. Instantly he hit is head in despair and said loudly, "Oh God, I would have to slip again today!"

Several people find this funny: why couldn't Mr Truman avoid stepping on the peel? Couldn't he exercise his brain a little bit? When we say that we have a habit of saying 'yes' and can't say 'no' when we choose to, we are being the Mr Truman of the twenty-first century, refusing to exercise our brain. We need to understand that the only way to break a habit is by conscious choice. It may be difficult to say 'no' when you don't want to say 'yes', but over a period of time the conviction to follow your inner instinct will set in, making your stand easier. It would also aid in making decisions based on your own mental analysis rather than the influence of external factors such as fears, peer pressure, etc.

So how do you say 'no' without hurting the other person's feelings or being overcome by guilt yourself? Many peole get sucked into the abyss because of various fears, such as being perceived selfish or lazy, or being mistaken for someone not ambitious or career driven, or even insensitive and unconcerned, but overcoming these fears by rationalizing them with clarity of purpose will put all of these doubts to rest. If giving in to these fears is what makes you a star at the office or the hero in your family, then you need to think again. People often fail to stand their ground as a means to get attention or recognition, but its presonal implications in the long run can be fatal. In the beginning one needs to consciously remind oneself to not say 'yes' when you want to say 'no', and before long it turns into a habit simplifying your life in more ways than one. Once you have accepted that you have the right (and often responsibility) to turn someone down, you can do it in a way that doesn't seem like a rejection. The best way to say 'no' is by being honest, and explaining it clearly. There are several tactful ways to the do the same in business situations also. I made a mental note to include them in the time mastery resource manual I would gift to Bobby later.

Rule 3: Do the right thing

In the words of management guru Peter Drucker, doing the *right thing* is more important than doing *things right*. We squander most of our time on a host of activities but achieve little because we do not concentrate on the right things. To be able to do that, we must first identify our core skills that are unique to each one of us. Subsequently, we must work around these core skills and take time out to enhance their value.

To cite an example, if your core skill lies in advertising, shift to advertising instead of whiling away your time on information technology. You would be wasting double the time doing something which is not your core skill and achieving just half the results.

The same principles that result in a successful business apply to time mastery as well. Like in business the 'right man for the right job' ensures maximum productivity, in life finding your core skill set and honing your talent in the same will ensure optimum performance with adequate effort. You need to take positive steps to not allow external factors such as popular belief or influence from family, friends, etc. to cloud your judgement in identifying and subsequently adapting your core-skill set. Only 10 per cent of people have the necessary focus and energy to do that naturally.

"Would you care for some refreshments, sir?" Both Bobby and I turned at the same time. A lean and unusually tall steward in a crisp freshly starched uniform stood behind us with a customary smile on his face. "Clear soup if it's possible, please." I said turning to Bobby for his preference. "Same for me," he said. The steward whispered a polite "Sure, Sir" and made his way to the main kitchen while we turned back to our discussion.

I said "Let me share the story of Tony with you. He did his masters in electrical engineering from a renowned university in the United States. He hunted for a job in the telecom industry for almost four months. Although he had the necessary background for the telecom industry, his interest and passion lay in sales and connecting with people. He spent a lot of time comparing between a career in business or electrical engineering, but eventually decided to set up a store selling electronics in wholesale. He is now doing great in business and is already a millionaire. The moral of the story is that when you move in an area that is aligned with your core interest, you begin to enjoy your work and results start pouring in. Work ceases to be work in the traditional sense and turns into a passion.

Rule 4: Be outstanding, not a perfectionist

We covered three important principles of time mastery. The sun would go down in an hour's time. Bobby wanted to go for a walk in the woods. He asked me if I wanted to come along and I said yes. Why would anyone say no for an energizing walk? "Bobby, what do you think about the new Microsoft Windows 2005 release?"

"I think it's great, it gets my job done. It has fewer bugs than Windows 2003 and crashes rarely; Microsoft has come a long way since Windows 95, but it has much longer way to go. There are a million places they could still improve," said Bobby.

I am a perfectionist.

"If the company had waited till the product reached perfection before launching it, the company wouldn't be where

MASTER THE BASIC RULES

it is today. Microsoft is the largest software company because it focused on producing outstanding software, rather than a perfect one. The Windows operating system, be it 95 or 98 or successive versions, was far from perfect, but was the best solution available in the market then. The Windows 2005 as we use it today evolved through a series of improvements and upgradations.

"The message here is that be it an individual or a company, the focus should be on producing outstanding and not necessarily perfect results. Nobody can be perfect, and no one needs to be as there is always scope for improvement."

"But how do you know the boundary between outstanding and perfection?" asked Bobby.

I did not know how to answer that, but I did know that having the awareness to differentiate between outstanding efforts and aiming for perfection was essential. At that moment, I did recall a story my dramatics professor had told me that related to this question. There was once a theatre director known for his talent. He would put in hard work to produce outstanding plays. As he grew older, he started striving for perfection. A good example of his perfection was that while rehearsing, he would himself move the chair by an inch to the right, then a couple of inches to the back, then again to the right and so on. Everyone loved his dedication towards his work, but as time passed his plays were perpetually delayed because of specifics like the chair alignment. This compromised the actors' performance as he didn't get enough time to rehearse. The moral of the story is: the director did well till he focused on producing outstanding plays, but failed the moment he got obsessed with perfection.

Remember the character of Julia Robert's husband in *Sleeping with the Enemy*, probably one of the best representations of how being a perfectionist does not always do you good. People look at perfectionism as nitpicking. Not that it should matter how others perceive us, but perfectionists usually see their responsibilities as burdens, making it more difficult for them to accomplish tasks in time. They start many tasks, but put off its completion until it meets their standards for perfection. However, these standards are most likely not recognized or appreciated by others while the perfectionist has wasted much time to accomplish the unnecessary. The person could strive for excellence rather than perfection. Excellence is defined as 'very good of its kind' or 'high-quality performance'. Perfection is defined as 'the condition of being flawless' which is not impossible, but most unlikely to achieve. Focus on what is realistic rather than ideal. Do the best you can in the time allowed. The time investment should be in proportion to the magnitude of the task or project at hand. Not that one should do a sloppy job, but focusing on doing things within a predetermined deadline is always better.

I was sure Bobby was much clearer about the distinction between being outstanding and being a perfectionist. I saw him nodding his head with his eyes closed. This understanding relieved him of the self-generated pressure he had built for himself at work. He felt his body become lighter instantly.

Rule 5: Spend 80 per cent of time on important but not urgent activities

We came back from the walk just before dark and went for dinner. Post dinner, I called home and spoke to Monica and Sunny. They were spending the night at Monica's parents' home and Sunny was having a good time with his grandparents. Bobby stepped in the moment I hung up.

"I see that you regularly speak to your family during trips," commented Bobby.

I know that independent of how busy I am during business trips, if I don't speak to Sunny and Monica often, I would end up spending a lot more time in explanations later."

Bobby Smiled.

I realized that unknowingly we had moved onto the fifth rule. This rule involves differentiating between *important* and *urgent* things. It is crucial to spend most of your time in doing important rather than urgent tasks. It is also essential to understand that truly urgent tasks can be dealt with, but it is the important things that when not attended to become urgent over time.

	Urgent	Not Urgent
Important	I ► Crises ► Pressing problems ► Firefighting ► Major scrap and rework ► Deadline-driven projects	II ► Prevention ► *Production capability* activities ► Relationship building ► Recognizing new opportunities ► Planning ► Re-creation
Not Important	III ► Interruptions ► Some calls ► Some mail ► Some reports ► Some meetings ► Proximate pressing matters ► Popular activities ► Some scrap & rework	IV ► Trivia ► Busywork ► Some mail ► Some phone calls ► Time-wasters ► Pleasant activities

Urgent and important

The best metaphor for understanding the importance of preventing an important task becomeing an urgent one comes from the scientific experiment done on frogs sometime in the late 1970s. At the time, scientists were experimenting on frogs for a noble cause (although cruelty on animals cannot be justified). During the experiments, scientists found that when they put a frog in a pot of boiling water, it leapt out immediately to escape danger. But when they put the same frog in a kettle filled with cool and pleasant water, the frog settled down. They gradually heated the kettle until it started to boil; the frog was unable to escape and died inside the kettle. It did not become aware of the threat until it was too late. The frog's survival instincts are geared towards detecting sudden changes.

We humans follow similar behaviour as frogs. Our instincts help us prepare and survive immediate changes in the environment. Try throwing a stone at someone and see if their hand instinctively catches it without letting it hurt them. We fail in circumstances where the issues creep up insidiously and became gigantic over time. One may have heard of statements like 'Boy, I didn't see that one coming.' Well, the reality is that even though we may see it coming, we choose not to give enough attention to take any action for that moment. We wait for the issue to escalate; till it becomes urgent often requiring a lot more time, effort and resources to deal with at the moment than earlier.

Seth Godin, author of *Unleashing the Idea Virus*, gives a perfect example. Let's examine two ways to catch a flight. The first way, which happens to be the most common one, is to leave on time, do your best to park as near as possible to the entrance, repeatedly glance at your watch, and then quicken your pace. When you get to security, you realize that you're quite late, so you cut the line shouting "My plane leaves in 10 minutes!" You walk faster, as you get closer to the gate, you realize that walking fast isn't working, so you start to jog. Three gates away, you break into a run, and if you're lucky, you make the flight in the nick of time.

The second way is to leave for the airport *10 minutes* early.

It is easy to avoid changes because of doubts, effort and apprehensions attached with it. Oftentimes the urgency of the situation forces us to take a decision and subsequent action that we would much rather avoid. You need to fight the urge to stay comfortably settled in a situation that may not be the best one. Another reason people shy away from adopting change is to avoid accepting responsibility for its consequences. In case things don't work out exactly as planned, we would rather blame the situation than accept responsibility for the change.

A study among business firms on the topic of parcel delivery reveals how organizations focus on urgent activities only. The study revealed that only 20 per cent of firms sent tax documents by regular mail, whereas 70 per cent sent them by overnight courier services and 10 per cent actually sent it by a personal messenger that is hundred times the cost of regular mail. Obviously, all that wasted money can be avoided. Companies spend millions every year on last-minute deliveries because like most of us, they confuse urgent with important.

Smart organizations and individuals work on the important to prevent it from turning urgent. Smart organizations understand that important issues are the ones to deal with. If you focus on the important stuff, the urgent will take care of itself.

Oftentimes, we use the urgent as an excuse for hurried work or hasty decision-making. A quick look at most countries' governments in spending money and resources when faced with an "emergency" reveals the same. Urgent is not an excuse. In fact, urgent is often an indictment, a sure sign that you've been putting off the important stuff until it is out of control.

The most important idea of all is that you will succeed in the face of change when you make the difficult decisions first. It is easy to justify racing for your flight when it is leaving in two minutes and you are five gates away. It is much harder to understand waking up 10 minutes early to avoid the problem altogether. Waking up early is the effective way to deal with the challenge. It may seem foolish to the person lying in bed next to you, but when you enjoy the benefits of a pleasant stroll to the gate, you realize that your difficult decision was a good one.

In our daily lives, there are many important tasks that we can handle in advance. It is critical that we became careful to watch the slowly changing trends in the environment, not just the sudden changes. It is a warning to be attentive to developing threats besides the obvious ones.

A simple approach to ensure that our focus stays on important tasks lies in planning. Planning forms the backbone of time mastery. It is a single-stop solution – total elimination of the feeling of being overwhelmed and ensuring maximum productivity. This single step can increase your productivity by 50 per cent or more.

One of the biggest time wasters is deciding what to do next. Even if we don't waste time in this activity, can we be sure that we picked a task that was more important than the other?

The solution lies in planning. Planning means structuring and preparing for the tasks at hand in a systematic, proactive manner. Planning does require time, but it sets the series of events and activities into organized motion. This smooth operation of a predetermined plan ensures fewer discrepencies and the ability to forsee potential problems, thereby reducing time needed for damage recovery or redoing certain tasks. Plan your day the night before. When you are clear about your outcomes for the next day, your subconscious goes to work in the night and figures out solutions while you are asleep.

You can plan your day, week or month in a manner that is most feasible for you. You could either plan in great detail or you could broadly outline the tasks at hand and set this in order for a specified period of time. This will ensure that you give adequate attention to the important things and not allow them to become urgent.

Rule 6: Focus on the 20 per cent tasks that account for 80 per cent of the results

This principle is based on a very important part of time mastery. It is called the Pareto principle which says that we need to consciously focus on the most important in a series of tasks which may be 20 per cent in number but bring in 80 per cent of the results. Often the matters low on the priority list take up most of all quality time compromising the quality of the task.

Consider things high on your list of priority as whales. These are the tasks which may be fewer in number but generate maximum results.

On the other hand the less important tasks can be classified as the smaller fish which are obviously large in number but don't bring as many results.

As a smart person your goal should be to first deal with the whales and then with the small fishes.

For example, while studying for an exam where the goal is to get good grades with limited time for study, it is helpful to understand the most important aspects in the curriculum and the psychology of the teacher setting the exam, rather than mindlessly mugging up the whole course. With careful thought and inspection, you would be able to cover 80 per cent of relevant course by studying 20 per cent of the most relevant material. Similarly, in case of work, it is important to complete the most important quality projects at the right time, instead of handling several low-quality projects of average impact. These so called 20 per cent of important projects would account for 80 per cent of your image that would contribute to your salary or promotion.

Rule 7: Make learning your friend

The thrill and other pleasure of familiarising yourself with something new constantly can be one of the best stimuli you can give your mind. This is why learning forms the very basis of human existence. A conscious will to learn can be both therapeutic as well as recreational to the mind. It enables us not to be trapped in a stoic state where there is absence of mental exercise or skill enhancement. The benefit of adopting a perpetual will to learn is tremendous and everlasting.

Learning can come from various sources, the most popular being books, seminars, teachers' trainings, workshops, private coaching, audio programmes, educational videos, practical experience, etc. Just imagine someone having a life experience of 10–20 years and sharing his learning through his book. When you read the book, you have advanced your knowledge and understanding by 10–20 years in that field. If you find yourself struggling with an issue, chances are that someone somewhere has already been in that situation before and has put the solution in the form of a book. Seminars and training programmes are also an excellent source of learning as they are interactive and without distractions. They represent total immersion learning; that is not only fun but also a form of maximum efficiency learning.

A classic example of displaying the power of learning is present in the use of 'Microsoft Office' (PowerPoint, Word, Excel, Outlook), all commonly used in any office setting. Some people take a learning class or try to understand it through someone. People hardly read the user manual as these tools look simple. But when one tries to give superior quality in a

PowerPoint presentation or a Word document, they spend a lot of time in figuring out how to carry out basic tasks such as adding an image or the alignment of text. They may eventually understand the important stuff by hit-and-trial method, but they could have saved plenty of time by simply taking a step to learn it.

Make learning your friend.

Post-Requisite – Execution and Discipline

Planning alone will not bear optimum results. It is equally important to execute those plans. Discipline yourself to complete tasks that you start. Any given task when performed continuously over a long stretch of time can be seen as cumbersome and boring. So it is helpful to switch horses mid-stream and break away from the prime task at reasonable intervals to refresh your mind and keep the energy levels up. For instance going back and forth between two subjects or projects may be good for breaking monotony; but it can also result in breaking the flow and lead to a loss of essence. Eventually, you may be too distracted to complete even one project properly. Keeping a balance is essential.

Execution of tasks is as important as planning itself. You may know many people who don't spend any time on planning, but there is a far greater number of people who plan but never execute. It calls for discipline and a sincere desire to keep commitments. Whenever you fail to execute as planned, get down to evaluate what went wrong.

Executing a plan often requires a deadline and deadlines can spell pressure for some people. However, this doesn't have to be the case. Pressure is not built into a deadline and it is not an objective reality either. "It seems that there's something 'subjective' ... There's some other way to relate to the deadline that reduces the pressure we feel," writes Stephen Randall in *Results in No Time*. He gives the example of what happens when someone puts his index fingers into the ends of a Chinese finger puzzle (a five-inch-long, woven hollow tube). "If you try to quickly pull your fingers out, then there's some pressure, and the puzzle turns into a trap. But if you simply relax, and simply get into the puzzle, moving your fingers closer together (getting more involved), there's no pressure, and the trap opens. The pressure we feel is directly proportional to how much we're resisting what we're doing," he explains. The implication is to learn to relax into a particular task and then concentrate all your energies on it, without getting distracted by other less important tasks (a feat that calls for a lot of mind disciplining).

Thus, time pressure depends primarily on our perspective; on the way we relate to a deadline. No matter what external causes we can identify, once we take on a job, I believe the pressure we feel is largely under our control. Even if you don't believe this, or are not sure about it, wouldn't it be a useful working hypothesis to test, to challenge yourself with?

Execution in contrast to strategic planning gets little intellectual respect. But even the most creative, visionary strategic planning is useless unless we translate it into action. Therefore, think about simplicity, clarity and focus; and review your progress relentlessly. That's the *mantra* for execution. The execution phase forces you to translate your broad-brush conceptual understanding into an intimate familiarity with how a project will happen; who will take on which tasks, and in what sequence; how long it will take to complete those tasks; how much it will cost; and how these tasks will affect subsequent activities.

Follow these steps for a flawless execution:

1. Let 'focus' be your buzzword

Always maintain your focus. You must constantly ask, "How realistic is this plan with my given resources?" Although it is a good idea to always stretch one's boundaries and do more than one thinks is possible, one must also be ready to test these goals against real possibilities. The idea is to reconcile the need for realism with the usefulness of stretched goals that help spur higher levels of performance. Just as reducing the sauce can help concentrate the flavour, distilling your strategy to its essentials can help deepen your understanding of the goals.

2. Develop tracking systems that facilitate problem-solving

Does the measure you are using tell you if you have accomplished the objective? Does the tracking system you have set up get to the heart of the problem you are trying to fix? Here is where precise thinking will pay big dividends. The right measure helps make expectations clear.

3. Periodically review your progress

The odds of successfully executing a plan that you don't review often are second to none. Keep your plan simple with an inbuilt review strategy. If you have a clear picture of the primary initiatives, as well as the key features that will impact your plan, you will have a better picture of your true progress.

Bobby had too much to assimilate after the marathon session. He had done little talking today. I was happy that he was mastering the art of listening!

6

State Management

"Imagine the beautiful landscape of the tallest snowcapped mountains. The sun has just risen, and the first rays of the sun are caressing the virgin snow. You can hear the melodious sound of the river even ten thousand feet above the river banks. This is a place where time stands still. On top of one of the smaller mountains, stands a sculptor. His name is Picasso. He has been living there for months at a stretch, working with his tools on a large block of solid ice. As he chisels in pursuit of a masterpiece, his mind focuses on the moment when this task would be complete. And the magical moment arrives. His beloved lifts the veil of his masterpiece, and the first warm rays of the sun pass through this magnificent piece of art, touching every curve of this statue.

"And this view my friend, is worth more than all the gold on Earth." I paused for a while narrating the story to Bobby, who was still visualizing the picture in his mind moments after the story had ended.

I continued after a long pause, "Bobby, certain pieces of art are invaluable, and it is even more valuable to be able to manage one's emotions. It would transform your life instantly, if you choose to implement it sincerely."

There was another long pause. Bobby was still coming out of the trance, trying to guess where I was leading him. I continued, "Bobby, remember the first rule in 'emotional mastery, which forms the root of time mastery, is to have a relaxed mind." I said.

Bobby accepted the idea with a pinch of salt, as was clear by the sudden sideways movement of his eyes.

He waited for me to speak further, and spoke himself when he realized that I had finished my statement. "John, you sound simple enough and I do realize the importance of a relaxed mind, but I'm not just sure I have the slightest clue on how to get there."

Bobby seemed discouraged because of his feeling of helplessness as far as mind control was concerned.

"Every time I think of work, or the ticking clock, my mind starts panicking. Doesn't everyone face this problem? Is it possible to have a relaxed mind at will, or is it a result of one's environment?" asked Bobby.

That was a fair question. It reminded me of this incident that happened between me and my dear Uncle Sam. Uncle Sam was about 55 years old, and was CEO and founder of a flourishing company. He was an excellent business leader, husband, father and a polo player but suffered from one serious problem. He was perpetually overwhelmed. Whenever you met him anywhere he would complain about all the work he had to do. He had a heart condition and the doctor said a change in mindset as well as lifestyle was essential. It still didn't have any effect on him. One day I visited him at home and he seemed to have gone through a massive transformation. He was extra cheerful and talked about his son's promotion. He did not say a single word about his work. I was happy and curious at the same time about what brought about this transformation. I

STATE MANAGEMENT

asked him what it is that had changed his life. He was happy to share his story.

> Last Monday, I came back home from work after a rough day. I told my wife Julie about the work that needed to be done and the consequences it would have in case it wasn't.
>
> Perhaps for the first time in our married life of 30 years, Julie stopped me in between and asked me "Honey, do you remember the first day when we got married and came to live with your parents? When I entered the house, the first thing I saw was the kitchen and a pile of dirty dishes in the kitchen. On that day, if I had stopped to think that over the course of the next 30 years, I would have to clean a million dishes, I would have given you a divorce then and there."
>
> I was puzzled. I was not sure what Julie was trying to point out. I managed to ask, "Darling, why would you ever focus on 30 years of washing dishes; shouldn't you focus more on the positives. Take life on a day-to-day basis. Of course you will ==feel overwhelmed if you focus on all the work you have to do in an entire lifetime.==”
>
> Julie's answer to this question brought about a transformation in my life. She answered, "Darling, isn't that what you do? Don't you focus on problems that can potentially come in your business the coming week, the coming month, the coming year or even a lifetime? I know you don't do it deliberately, but that is exactly what you do. I can never understand either why any person would do it, let alone someone who has had two heart attacks. You tell me Sam, how is this different from focusing on 30 years of washing dishes which you commented on a moment ago?"
>
> And that set me thinking. It was only a matter of days when a new Uncle Sam was born.

After sharing this story, I turned my attention to Bobby. He had probably understood the message, but I thought that I would give him a little more to be sure. "Bobby, it is our focus that determines a relaxed mind or an overwhelmed state. Focusing on everything that can go wrong will make a person overwhelmed. Keeping one's mind stable and focusing on the positive will keep the mind relaxed enabling the person to solve the problems that lie ahead in a better way."

I noticed that Bobby's ears were glued to my talk, but he focused his attention on the deer running at a distance, as visible from our cottage. The deer was running back and forth for no apparent reason. It seemed that Bobby was not looking at the deer, but was in deep thought, as if trying to remember or comprehend something. After about five minutes of silence, Bobby stood up and started pacing back and forth in the room. He looked at me and broke the silence. "You are absolutely right, John. Now that you say it, it all makes sense. If I look at times in my life when I felt overwhelmed, it had nothing to do with the situation I was in. For I have been tensed even during the best times in my life. I specifically remember this time when I had just got a promotion, was feeling fit and perfectly healthy, was enjoying a rejuvenated relationship with my wife; and everything in life was going smoothly." Bobby continued after a slight pause and a changed tone. "Except that my son was not getting good grades in school.

"And I constantly focused my attention on how much time I needed to take out from my already busy schedule, to be able to help my son over the next semester. This made me constantly overwhelmed and it started affecting other areas of my life as well. On the other hand, if I had chosen to look at the positives, and taken life by even 'one lesson a week' for my son, I would have helped him improve his grades, and simplified my life as well. I transferred my negative state to my son and ended up hurting his grades even more. It affected my performance in office too as I was constantly thinking about it.

"John, had I known that solution to my problem is so simple, I would have implemented it there and then."

"It's never too late Bobby. Now would be an excellent time to start focusing on the positives and choose to focus on one task at a time ensuring we do all of these tasks with a relaxed mind."

I didn't have to say anything more. Suddenly, I noticed that even I was staring at the mesmerizing deer. The deer was alone with nature; there was a bonding, a sense of harmony on another plain. It was playing with the trees, the bushes and the green grass, the fresh air and the blue sky. Some clouds were still visible in the sky reminding us of the showers we received a couple of days ago. The deer was moving in no particular direction, in giant graceful leaps. It seemed to have a great time. Clearly, the deer understood the meaning of living in the now, not past or future. Being present in the moment happens to be the best means to have control over one's emotional state. If one has complete control over their 'state', and by 'state' I mean the balance that exists between one's mind and body, then one's success is guaranteed. I remembered that I had learnt a technique in the seminar that changed my state instantly. I decided to try the state-changing exercise on Bobby.

"Stand up," I said firmly.

Bobby stood up. "I am sure you, like everyone else, may sometimes get into a negative state where you just don't feel like doing anything. Maybe you get into such a state rarely, but it does hamper your life significantly then. You know that it is not right, but are not sure why exactly you feel low or what you can do to change it."

"Bobby, what do you do to change your state at that moment?" I asked.

"A few times," Bobby said looking at me from the corner of his eye. He continued, "I do get into a negative state every now and then, that is a few times in an hour."

He gave me a mock smile. After giving some thought, he continued with his expression. "Now that I think about it, I used to smoke a cigarette to change my state till my doctor put a strict ban due to a problem with my lung. Now I watch television for hours whenever I feel that I am not in the zone. Rita goes shopping whenever she feels she needs to be eased of her daily pressures, even though I can't say it is easy on my wallet or my blood pressure." He was smiling again.

The power move

"Bobby, I am going to teach you a magic formula to change your state instantly without the need to use an external substance. I call it the 'power move', some people call it 'whoosh'. All that you need to do is to stand straight and fold your fingers into a fist. Then move your hand very fast, while saying the magical word 'yes', bending a little and getting your whole body involved in the exercise. It is the same movement you would do after coming out of an exam hall or a match, where you know you have performed well and can expect excellent results. A simple movement like this can go a long way in changing both your mental and physical state."

I stood up and demonstrated the move to Bobby, and then we did the move again together. The intensity of our 'yes' was so loud that it scared the deer away.

Now that we were both feeling excited, rejuvenated and energetic, it was time to introduce peak state performance.

Peak state performance has many definitions, but for simplicity sake, I define it as a state in which an individual is able to get 80 per cent or higher results of his or her maximum capacity. Massively successful people remain in their peak states most of the time and not just when they are performing a feat. Michael Jordan, the star basketball player revealed in an interview that his success was attributed to his taking every practice as if it were the NBA finals. One can infer that he was always in a peak state of mind and body. Success in examinations is also a result of a perpetual peak state.

Bobby knew about peak state performance, but had a problem in its application. To him, this idea was theoretically sound, but he wasn't convinced if it was posible to stay in a constant peak performance state in practical life. My answer is simple – you can remain and perform in a peak state simply by choosing to do so by making a commitment to yourself. Once you commit that you will work only when you are in a peak state, you will find ways to remain in that state all the time. You can always come back to the peak state again to finish the work in an overall less amount of time. The power move is a handy tool to bring you to this peak state of mind and body.

> Remember, *how much* you work does matter, but not as much as *how* you work. This is what distinguishes achievers from the others. Peak state performance should be your central idea while doing any act.

Although Bobby related with most of what I was saying, it seemed that something was troubling him. There was this boiling question in his mind, waiting to be unleashed. The question had been building pressure for a while now. Finally, he managed to sum up his thoughts and ask "John, I don't know if there is an answer to this question, but tell me if you can. How is it that during several phases of life, I eat well, exercise regularly, enjoy my job, love my partner, think positively – yet I often find myself in a negative mood? I feel angry, panic-stricken, guilty and depressed. This inconsistency gets me into a negative cycle where I drink and smoke regularly and even start to perform poorly at work. It often seems that I have no control over these emotions and this is seriously hampering my life."

I had some good news for Bobby. "The good news is that you can have full control over your emotions and there is a huge body of research that proves just that. Emotional mastery is possible with understanding the causes of emotional upheavals, subsequent changes and how we can consciously use this understanding to change the state from negative to positive. An 'anchor' explains how your mood can change in response to a trigger or a stimulus. Let's say you are watching a programme on TV. It flashes an advertisement for some snack food, and the next moment, you are heading for your refrigerator for some 'comfort food'. That's an example of anchoring. The advertisement (stimulus) immediately triggered a desire for food (response) in you."

Looking at Bobby didn't convince me if he had understood anchoring. I continued, "Let's take another example. Say someone close has died in your family. Undoubtedly, you are not in the best of your emotional state. You are standing at the funeral and one by one all the guests leave after the ceremony is over. As they leave, they pat you on your shoulder as a gesture of condolence. Your subconscious mind develops a link between the 'patting on shoulders' and a 'negative state'.

"Years later, you forget the incident and are having a good time at the party. One of your friends walks over to you and pats you on your shoulder, without any specific intent. You would immediately go into a negative state of mind, as subconsciously you link these two activities of shoulder tapping and the event of death (negative state) together. This is the power of anchors. The anchor will automatically and instantly propel you into an emotional state.

"Once we get a better understanding of our existing anchors, we can choose to break anchors that put us in a negative state and replace them with positive anchors that steer us to a positive state of mind. Breaking a negative anchor requires you to first identify the stimulus that causes a change in your emotional state and place a positive anchor in its place while acknowledging the cause of the change.

"Bobby, the easiest way to override a negative anchor is by forcing yourself into a peak state by using power moves. The power move is the best positive anchor. Creating a positive anchor is simpler than you would imagine. Whenever you are in a peak state, you can capture and reinforce the effect of those moments by attaching a unique stimulus like listening to a piece of classical music, or performing a unique motion like clapping in a certain way. By repeating this a couple of times, your brain will form a link between your peak state and the 'music' or the 'clapping sound'.

"Later, whenever you catch yourself slipping into a dark mood, play that piece of music, do the clapping or perform that power move; you will automatically feel transported to a different (more relaxed) state of mind. Sounds corny, but I recommend that you try it out on yourself. This phenomenon has roots in science and I have just two words for it, 'It Works'."

Bobby said, "I agree hundred per cent to what you are saying. You know, whenever I hear the music of *Titanic*, I get into a great state because I remember the time when I had first met my wife, and she was singing the song onstage. She looked at me in such a way that I fell in love instantly. On the other hand, I always go into a negative state when I smell the Hugo Boss perfume. Although I know that it's an excellent perfume, I once wore the perfume and had fallen terribly sick with fever. I couldn't bathe for three days and kept on smelling the perfume and feeling sick, the perfume was just anchored with a negative state then, even though I liked it a lot before.

"I must say I'm amazed. It actually feels like I've discovered a miracle cure for every ailment. What is more interesting is that I have the power to use it at my will. It doesn't matter what I'm going through, I need to attach a relevant anchor and I can change my state instantly. Can I anchor the positive air around us now and use it the next time I'm not in a peak performance state?" said Bobby.

"Sure," I answered smilingly. Bobby had now started to ask questions of a better quality. The kind of questions we ask ourselves determine our emotional state, and our destiny. It reminded me of an incident that took place with Swami Parthasarthy:

A man approached Swami Parthasarthy and put the following question to the learned seer: "Swamiji, a company has released an appointment advertisement for the post of a CEO and a clerk. Which position should I apply for?" The Swami's answer was "clerk", because a person who qualifies to apply for a CEO's post won't ever have asked this question, in the first place!

While Bobby was still chewing on this eternal truth about questions, I approached the subject in a more direct fashion. "Bobby, the inference of this story is: the quality of questions we ask, either of ourselves or others, controls the quality of our lives. It's the questions we ask our mind that shape up our emotional well-being, and eventually our entire life."

I remember a time when nothing seemed to work in my life. And I asked the following obvious question, 'Why is this happening to me?' I got several answers to the question, like: 'Maybe it is the result of some bad karma in the past' or 'Maybe I am just plain dumb!' This offered me a justification, but it didn't help in improving my state. With time, I realized that the answers weren't wrong; I was just asking the wrong questions. I could have asked a different question like, 'How can I do better next time?' and get all the right answers, which would help me.

I am confident that once we consciously start asking these empowering questions, instead of demoralizing ones, we would develop the art of asking good questions and coming up with equally good answers. The questions we ask ourselves would improve with the quality of experiences we have and will steer us to ultimate success.

The ringing phone broke my thought process. I picked up the phone to hear the loveliest voice on the other side. "How are you darling?" I looked at Bobby and said in almost a mute voice, "It's Monica. Give me five minutes."

"Sure," answered Bobby.

Bobby left the room. When he came back, his face suggested that he had something to tell me. "You know John, I just realized what spoils my whole day. Generally, when I wake up in the morning, my first question is 'Why do I need to wake up?' or 'Do I have to do this?' or 'Couldn't I sleep for just five more minutes?' These questions intensify negative feeling towards work, and that is how I feel the whole day. Now that I know it's the questions that control my feelings, if I were to change the questions, I can change my feelings. I have decided that from now on, when I wake up, I am going to ask some new questions."

"Questions like . . ." I interfered.

"Well questions like, *'How excited can I be today?' 'What all good stuff will I be doing today?' 'How energetic am I going to feel the whole day?'*" he answered.

And I knew that he was on the right track.

7

Outcome-Oriented Planning

It was 7 a.m. and the warm rays of the sun falling through the window promised a clear sky throughout the day. Bobby stepped in wearing his usual blue jeans and white t-shirt. He had an aura of newfound energy, a joy that comes from discovering something wonderful. I noticed his posture was different this morning, and the restlessness in his stance clearly showed his enthusiasm to get started.

I didn't want him to waste time either. We only had an hour before we went for breakfast. The rest of the day had a series of meetings lined up. We were going to discuss planning today. Planning excited me as it forms the backbone of time mastery.

I was going to discuss the W5H planning method. A method where you focus on the Which? What? Why? When? Who? and How? of an outcome/result at hand.

Traditional planning methods like the To Do lists focus on the actions. What is to be done is the sole focus of To Do lists. For example, the To Do list may have activities like: *buy bread from Modern Bakers, go to car mechanic's shop, pick up child from school, take client to dinner at the fancy restaurant across from office, file my receipts, prepare for the presentation to be given to boss, workout with Bob, call up Sam* and so on.

Traditional planning

Now don't get me wrong. I agree that the To Do list is an excellent first step in planning serving as a written record of things and helping reduce a lot of stress. It will be much harder to manage and acomplish all the tasks at hand if we rely on our memory alone especially when an average person performs over fifty activities a day! As a beginner in planning, To Do list is a recomended methodology.

However, many a time these very To Do lists can be overwhelming. The lists may continue to grow at a much quicker pace than the speed with which we can get the tasks done. We may have a feeling that we are never able to finish what we have on our plate if we fail to cross everything on the To Do list. We become so focused on crossing off items in our lists that the execution process becomes robotic and lacks enthusiasm. A classic example would be a person having 'buying flowers for my wife' as a To Do item. He may execute the task, without feeling any joy in doing so unless he focuses on the purpose of this action.

Many a time we forget the true purpose behind the task and we may either do it half-heartedly or keep postponing the task for ever.

The solution to problems in traditional planning is focusing on the outcome/result first instead of the actions during the planning stage. The first question you need to ask is "Which outcome am I seeking for the day, week, month or long-term? Then ask the two questions – 'Why?', 'What?' – around the outcome. 'What?' refers to the set of actions that need to be done to achieve the outcome. 'Why?' refers to the purpose of the result, why is it that we wish to achieve that outcome. Let us take the following example:

W5H planning

make to do list more effective by compelling by [ACTION / OUTCOME / PURPOSE]

OUTCOME-ORIENTED PLANNING

(Actions) To Do List

1. File my receipts
2. Prepare for the presentation
3. Work out

If we were to recreate the list in terms of the W5H planning method, the new list may look like the following:

Action	File my receipts
Outcome	Completely up-to-date with tax-info for 2005
Purpose	To be financially independent within the next five years
Action	Prepare for the presentation
Outcome	To deliver an outstanding lecture on time mastery
Purpose	To assist people in living the lives of their dreams
Action	Work out at the gym
Outcome	To maintain and enhance my current fitness levels
Purpose	To live each day filled with energy and vitality

In the context of their outcome and purpose, each task now has greater meaning and is easier to approach with a sound mind and a clear line of thought. Thus, we can instantly make our To Do lists a thousand times more compelling by connecting each action on the list to both the specific outcome it is designed to achieve and the more general purpose it is moving you towards.

> "The purpose of life is a life of purpose."
> —Robert Byrne

Now the W5H is not just a fancy way of making a To Do list, it is a way of making a psychology shift. In real life, we should not be thinking of 'actions' first and then justify them with 'outcome' and 'purpose'. Rather we should first focus on the outcomes and the purpose of our life; the actions would surely follow. Let us take an example where we are clear about some of the outcomes we wish to achieve in the near future.

Outcome
1. Buy a beachfront property somewhere exotic
2. Meet someone I'd like to spend the rest of my life with

Now, here is what it looks like when we expand these outcomes using, 'why' we are looking for a particular outcome and 'what' actions do we need to take to achieve them.

Outcome	Buy a beachfront property somewhere exotic
Purpose	To live a life of ease
Action(s)	A. Work between four and six hours a day on my business
	B. Explore retirement options
	C. Research long-term investment opportunities
Outcome	Meet someone I'd like to spend the rest of my life with
Purpose	To live a life filled with love and create a family
Action(s)	A. Work on loving myself first
	B. Read *Attracting Genuine Love*
	C. Get into great physical condition

If we form a habit of delivering the outcome first, the time spent in execution of actions would be much simpler and perfectly relevant. Just in case an action doesn't accomplish the task, we need not worry about it as we can always think of a different 'action' to achieve the same outcome. For example, if the book *Attracting Genuine Love* was not available anywhere in the market, I could form an alternative strategy, such as: read any other book on the same subject, or seek advice from someone who has either read the book or has the necessary experience. There are always a <u>number of ways</u> to <u>achieve the same outcome</u>. Here, we choose the most feasible 'action' to accomplish a particular 'outcome' and thus save time.

The purpose forms the motivation for the action. The reason people begin several tasks but often fail to finish them is because during the process, <u>they lose the purpose of the outcome in the first place</u>. I learnt this lesson by listening to the story of an Indian saint.

> There was an Indian saint named Mullah Nassurudin. He was travelling in a train when the ticket checker came in to check tickets. His attention went directly to Mullah Nassurudin, who looked like an old beggar. He was seated at the last seat in the train compartment and was looking tensed. Mullah was putting his hands in his pockets, acting as if he was trying to find something. He looked like someone panic-stricken; and beads of sweat were visible on his forehead. The ticket checker had several years of experience in his profession, and by now he could easily guess who had a ticket and who didn't, and Mullah fell in the latter category. As the ticker checker approached Mullah and asked for the ticket, Mullah became even more tensed. He searched his pockets and produced a ticket. The ticket checker looked at it and found that it was a valid ticket. He asked Mullah about why he was so tensed when he had the ticket. Mullah replied, "Son, I always knew I had the ticket. But I had forgotten my destination.

> I was trying to find the ticket to remind myself where I was going."

How often does it happen that you forget the destination, and mindlessly work on the outcome? The purpose is equally important as the action.

To summarize, in life, it is useful to approach a situation in the following manner – Which (Outcome), Why (Purpose), What (Action).

> *For several enlightened souls, who have a clear purpose in life, they can work the equation backwards. Here's how it works:*
>
> *Purpose: To love, to serve, and to give of my abundance*
>
> *Outcome 1: Create a loving home*
>
> *Action 1: Spend the afternoon with my family*
>
> *Action/Outcome: Volunteer at my local church or community centre/ To become more connected to my community*
>
> *Action/Outcome: Donate 10 per cent of my February income to the Tsunami relief fund/Experience my abundance more fully*
>
> *By focusing on the actions you can take to manifest your purpose and the outcomes you intend those actions to engender, you translate a worthy purpose into a worthwhile life.*

Several times throughout the day, ask yourself why you are doing whatever you are doing. Be sure to begin your answer with a phrase like 'in order to', 'so that', or 'for the purpose of'. If you realize that your activity is purposeless, stop doing it! If the activity seems purposeless but you cannot or will not stop doing it, ask yourself why you would choose to do it. When you have generated at least three possible purposes, choose the one which feels most inspiring to you.

Have fun with the process; with W5H you can focus on the outcomes and live a life of purpose! Don't get confused if something is an outcome or action, whatever feels right is the right thing.

You may be wondering what happened to the other two Ws and the H, as the name of the planning technique was W5H, and till now we have discussed only the 'Which', 'What' and the 'Why'. The other two Ws in the planning technique stand for two more important questions, namely the 'When' and the 'Who'. 'When' simply stands for the deadline by when the task needs to be completed. A significant task would have a predetermined deadline. Not that every task needs to be time-bound, it is better to attach some time frames to each outcome or action. However, one has to keep in mind the dynamics of an activity and make changes accordingly.

The least understood of all the Ws in the W5H planning method is the 'Who'. For when we create To Do lists, we always assume that it is we who will be executing it. In the W5H planning method, the 'Who' plays the most important role in achieving the outcome. It requires understanding the art of getting things done through the efforts of other people. This doesn't mean that you are no longer accountable at large, you still have the responsibility of the final outcome in spite of the inputs by other appropriate people or in simple words, results of the delegated work.

Some people understand delegation as giving work and forgetting about it, hoping the work will happen by itself. Many people delegate work, get hurt and then take a vow never to delegate work ever again and do all the work themselves.

To be successful and get a sense of fulfilment, it is essential to learn the art of getting work carried out by someone, where you focus only on certain core areas. These are the things you alone can do in a given set-up. A practical bottleneck can occur when you fail to get the desired outcome from the people you delegated parts of the task to. This could be due to various reasons – lack of wholesome communication, incorrect job assignment, impractical deadlines, novelty of tasks, incomplete induction, inadequate training, etc. A dependable solution to this problem can be the establishment of a process with clear lines of execution and their outcomes. This system with its simplicity and transparency would enable even a less skilled person to achieve the required results.

The last but important element in W5H planning process is the 'How'. 'How' refers to a detailed step-by-step execution strategy of the actions we intend to take to achieve a particular outcome. We should form a strategy based on experience or in consultation with a sound and dependable source.

* * *

Suddenly, the phone rang. I came back to my senses. The phone bell died before we could pick up the receiver. I looked at Bobby, I must have been looking a little lost for Bobby to have that expression on his face. "Bobby, were we in a conversation since the . . ." I looked at my watch and continued, "the last hour."

"We were not in a conversation, but you were. It seemed you were talking to yourself, in deep thoughts and speaking them aloud. I didn't interrupt you as I could relate to everything you said." I wanted to hear more of Bobby's thoughts, but didn't have much time as we had to leave for breakfast.

Breakfast was great. Fruit juices, museli and breads of over 35 varieties. Interestingly, bread was a speciality of this place, as was clear from the several choices available. The sumptuous breakfast was followed by a long meeting with only a few breaks and it was 8.30 p.m. when we ended. It is hard to believe that time passed quickly when you are doing things you enjoy.

We didn't have much time after dinner and decided to start the next session the next day. I wanted to ensure that he understands the power and benefits of this concept. While walking back towards our rooms, I asked him "Bobby, how do you think the W5H Planning method will benefit you?"

"Benefit?" he exclaimed, "this will transform my life. You have opened my eyes. I just realized what I had been missing for so long. As for my life, I've been doing things, deriving no juice whatsoever. In fact I didn't know why I was doing most of these things. I guess I just conformed to what everyone else was doing. I never knew that the simplest, most mundane activities can be exciting and rewarding in the long run. Suddenly, changing diapers with Rita in the middle of the night begins to sound not so bad. I realize that once I am clear about the purpose and focus on the outcome, I can actually enjoy myself. After all, life happens but once. If I must spend a major portion of it doing the routine things, I might as well make the most of it. I surely don't want to look back one day and reminisce a life of discontent and regret if I can seriously apply things we talked about in my life, I'm certain life can be a pleasure despite the occasional pain.

"John, like you said, I understand that W5H is not just a planning process, it is a shift in psychology. Unless even Bill Gates of Microsoft focuses on the outcome and purpose of his actions, his tasks would be as routine as most people in the world, where all the time goes in meetings, charity, planning, motivating employees and so on. In life, the real juice comes from the desired outcome, and to achieve that we need to stay focused. Well, now I know where to focus my energy.

"I know what I was missing in my planning process. You know John, my first job was of a call centre executive where I sold life insurance. My sole focus during that time was strictly on the action – to make calls. I had a target of ten calls an hour, so I was caught up in achieving my target and failed to focus on the main outcome, that is, closing the deal. Had I been clear about that, I would have mastered the script a little more and selected more wisely from my database. I know I could have done a much better job back then. Anyway I intend to be even better now. I would have also made a positive selection on my database so the conversion likelihood would have been higher. I know I can't go back in life to revert it, but I can implement it in my life now.

"The other day, I had 'buying flowers for Rita', my wife, on my To Do list, but all the flowers in the city were sold out. I wasn't sure what to do; I kept looking around for a couple of hours. When I didn't succeed, I finally ordered them on the internet paying 10 times the cost. Not that I regret the money as my wife is the love of my life, but I see now that I had forgotten the outcome and purpose. The outcome from that act was 'to see the smile on Rita's face' and the purpose was 'to strengthen our lasting relationship'. I could have achieved the same outcome buying her a 'lip gloss'. You wouldn't believe how much she loves 'lip gloss'. She wasn't even happy when she realized how much I had spent on the flowers, especially because my tone suggested how much of a favour I was doing in buying such costly flowers. Whereas a lip gloss would have meant that I had put in thought on what she cared about, and taken action accordingly. Hmm . . . if only I had focused on the outcomes instead of the actions, our relationship would have been so different today.

"But nothing is lost I guess, we still have time to make up, especially with my newly-learnt wisdom. What do you say John?" he said looking at me half smiling half crying. He was clearly nostalgic and thinking about Rita.

I looked at him with a thumbs up! I realized we had been talking, or rather Bobby had been talking for over 15 minutes while we were standing at the door of my room. I said good night, went to my room and fell asleep.

When I woke up, I thought about how outcome-oriented planning had transformed my life. I was confident that Bobby had understood the importance of planning with a strong focus on the outcomes instead of the actions and would implement it. Next he needed to understand prioritizing outcomes. I followed a prioritization system based on how much we valued specific areas of our life including career, family, etc. and referred to it as 'value-based prioritization'.

8

Value-Oriented Prioritization

"Would that be all sir?" said the steward as he cleared the trays of fresh orange juice and cereal.

"Yes please, and could you send some mixed nuts around 11 by the golf course, that's where the meetings will be held today." Bobby was excited about the day for two reasons. One, he felt the outdoor setting was perfect stimulation for his mind, and two, it was the sixth day of the conference, which meant he would be seeing Rita and his son soon. He missed them terribly, especially Rita, for he couldn't wait to share his newfound wisdom with his wife.

Bobby hastened his steps towards the golf course as he made mental notes of what lay ahead in the day. The itinerary was crucial. During the course of the conference several plans were made, several strategies formed and several decisions taken. What was important now was to set them in order of priority so the team knew where to focus on the basis of productivity and significance.

"Good morning," Bobby chirped as he approached John, who was ready to take a set by the perfect theatre-style setting on the freshly mowed grass.

VALUE-ORIENTED PRIORITIZATION

"Good morning. I think it will be a few minutes before we get started," I said.

We chatted for a while before his assistant called for everyone's attention. The next two hours were spent in enthusiastic discussions, with doses of disagreement among various participants. The goal was to reach a unanimous opinion on the major activities that lay ahead.

"So if we associate the word 'value' with priority, what would lie higher in your value system, higher profits or higher customer satisfaction?" I asked the group.

"Customer satisfaction definitely, if the customer is happy, profits would follow," was the spontaneous response from the group. A unanimous agreement always sounded like music.

Needless to say that the day was a fruitful one. The resort always had a special feel in the evenings. The trails leading to our cottatges were lit up with coloured glass lights in the floor. The air smelt of jasmines and there was a slight nip in the air.

"Monica would like it here," I thought as I made my way to join Bobby by the pool. We ordered tall glasses of iced tea and settled in for a relaxing chat.

"Bobby, what do you think steers the course of our life, governs our thoughts, leads our actions?" I asked.

Bobby looked at me with a slightly dazed expression. It was obvious that the answer required a good amount of thought.

"Well a whole lot of things, I guess," he answered. "What if you were to name a few?" I asked. "Okay . . . but you must know I have never consciously given it much thought" Bobby answered. I could see the desperation in his eyes as he seeked my help with the answer.

"Let me simplify the question, what forms the basis of how we lead our lives, the motivating factors behind what we do and why we do them? The labels, so to speak, of the things which govern our lifestyles."

Bobby leaned back his chair and said "Happiness, family, financial freedom, comfort . . . I could go on."

"Good. Different things work for different people, and all of them can be classified under a pain or pleasure state we experience through them in life. Simply put, some things that have a pleasurable effect on us and we attach a positive connotation to may be labelled as a positive value and would obviously be rated high on our value system. For example, family, independence, travel, success and commitment are generally clubbed under the pleasure state. However, a couple of things listed above can spell pain for some people. For instance commitment may not feature high on someone's value system if they associate commitment with being tied down. Similarly, travel could mean pain for someone who is a homebody or prefers being stationed at one place.

One can be in multiple pleasure states at the same time, e.g. being on a vacation at an exotic place can mean happiness, fulfil the need for being with family, reflect on success and financial freedom by virtue of being able to afford the holiday and strengthen your commitment to your partner if they accompany you.

"Makes sense" said Bobby with a Zen-like expression on his face and then continued. "But how can you relate pleasure, pain states with time mastery?"

"There is a connection, a significant one," I said. "One of the biggest reasons for wastage of time is indecision, and this indecisiveness comes from a lack of clarity in values or the things we classify under either pleasure or pain state. It is imperative that we clearly distinguish between the two. Our value system, or in other words, our way of prioritizing the labels that steer our life, needs to be clear. This will save the time in deciding what is important to us and what is not.

VALUE-ORIENTED PRIORITIZATION

Following this, focusing on what really matters would be much simpler."

I could see the keeness in Bobby's eyes. So I continued, "For example if a person's value system comprises both health as well as comfort, then one needs to prioritize the two. One way to do this would be to choose between an hour of exercise which benefits health or an extra hour of comfortable sleep. How we prioritize the two activities would give us a clear picture of what is more important, and we can subsequently invest our time on the same."

Bobby was listening to my explanations and decided to join in. "But John, I think I value **Health** more than **Comfort**, but continue to sleep. Why does it happen?"

I answered, "Well, the problem is that you think with your conscious mind and rate your values in a certain order, but it is the subconscious mind that decides all the actions. The subconscious mind may store your values differently than the conscious mind. So, if you feel your actions are not in line with your values, then your subconscious mind is in conflict with your conscious mind. Let's do a simple exercise. Let's write down all our values in a decreasing order of priority. For example, if you choose work over family, then **Career** is more important to you than **Family**. In case you are willing to skip meals or have a dozen cups of coffee to work more, then **Health** is lower than **Career** in your value system. In case you spend more time with your friends when compared with family, then **Friends** are higher in the value chain."

That set Bobby thinking. It amazed him to find out how his actions representing his value system in his subconscious mind were different from the ones in his conscious mind. He realized the discontent in his life was because of a clash of values. Awareness is the first step towards transformation.

o Affirmation associated with subconscious mind is important.

"I think I know now that I need to build a value system in my subconscious mind which is different from the one I have in my mind right now. How do I do it?" Bobby asked.

It was a simple yet powerful question. To begin with, awareness itself brings about a change in one's value system. To make the change permanent in one's subconscious mind, the simplest way is by taking actions you would have taken assuming you were to adopt a new value system. For example, if you start going for morning jog, then **Health** would become a priority over **Comfort**. If you start returning home on time to spend time with your family, or start to skip less important, useless company dinners to learn meditation and self-connection, then ***Fulfilment*** would became a priority over ***Work***.

It is important to remember that no particular value is superior to the other. Many so-called self-help gurus propagate that everyone must place **Family** over **Career**. But that is not necessarily true; everyone has the right to choose their own value system. What is more important is to consciously prioritize their value system rather than mindlessly accepting the ones that result from social conditioning. It is also essential to align our actions with the value system we wish to make a part of our daily life. We should make prioritization an integral and applicable part of our life, enabling us to decide easily whenever we have to pick between several activities. Being an efficient decision-maker would enable us to take a big leap towards becoming a master of time.

"Bobby, there is one recommendation I do want to make on what could be at the top of one's value system. I learnt it the hard way, but now I am convinced on what should be at the top of one's value system independent of age, sex or nationality. And that one value is **Health**. We take our health for granted, but when it bites back, it leaves us in no position to enjoy any

VALUE-ORIENTED PRIORITIZATION

other pleasure values. I didn't realize that till I had kidney stone problems at the age of 21 because of poor eating habits."

"It all makes sense John," blurted Bobby. "The reason I was a bad time manager was because of my <u>inability to decide on how to spend time</u>; which was because of <u>lack of clarity of my values</u>. My values were a result of conditioning and not the ones I consciously would have selected for me. So even if I would pick one activity, I would always wonder why I wasn't doing the other. Sometimes while working late at the office, I would think about family and while relaxing at home, I would think about office and my career. Now that I understand my values, I would be able to appreciate why I picked one activity over another at any given moment of time."

Values *Health* *Freedom* *Travel* *Family* *Friends* *Love* *Adventure* *Career* *Fun* *Success* *Fulfilment* *Security* *Outrageousness* *Comfort* *Contribution* *Commitment*	Vicky's current ranking 1. Health 2. Freedom 3. Travel 4. Adventure 5. Family 6. Friends 7. Success 8. _____	Bobby's current ranking (based on action) 1. Career 2. Success 3. _____	Bobby's proposed ranking 1. Health 2. Family 3. _____

91

It is also important to understand that prioritizing in the value system is not a static idea but changes over time. I had an uncle who was a career-driven person and whenever I met him, he would only talk about work and his career. I wouldn't let such an opportunity go by, and I told about him to John, who was the VP of our company then, regarding hiring him. John made an excellent offer and uncle decided to join our company. Uncle's performance was excellent, and I realized that I would always hire people who had career higher on their priority list.

Time passed by and Uncle grew older, I met him the other day and he told me that he had taken two months off from work. I was pleasantly surprised and inquired about what motivated him to do so. He told me that one of his closest childhood friends had come over from London and they were spending two months together all over the country. Now, that was unlike uncle. He noticed my curiosity and said, "Son, priorities in life change over time. Friends have now become more important to me in life, because the time I spend with them is what gives me all the joy and satisfaction in life." And that taught me a lesson I will always remember.

It is also important to realize that one can consciously change the value system with time and as the situation demands. For example, if you are unwell, you can consciously make health the topmost priority (unless that is already the case) till the time you heal. Or if you are just starting your career and want to make a mark, you may pick career as a high priority for a limited time thereby directing your decisions towards what is more important to your life at that time. It is important to follow any deadlines we may set for consciously changing the priorities in life.

For example, an activity such as playing tennis helps you be in several pleasure states like health, friends and even adventure at the same time. Taking your family on a business travel vacation can lead you to be in pleasure values like career, travel and family at the same time. To make the best use of your time, it is helpful to design activities that can enable you to experience several pleasure values at the same time, and then consciously make such activities a part of your life.

Sometimes we get so busy in making a living that we lose track of the purpose, which was designing a life and not making a living. It reminded me of this young man who worked with me at my previous office and how he learnt the most important thing in life from the guy next door.

> It had been some time since Tom had seen the old man. College, girls, career, and life itself got in the way. In fact, Tom moved across the country in pursuit of his dreams.
>
> There, in the rush of his busy life, Tom had little time to think about the past and often no time to spend with his wife and son. He was working on his future, and nothing could stop him.
>
> Over the phone, his mother told him, "Mr Weger died last night. The funeral is on Wednesday."
>
> Memories flashed through his mind like an old newsreel as he sat quietly remembering his childhood days.
>
> "Tom, did you hear me?"
>
> "Oh sorry mom. Yes, I heard you. It's been so long since I thought of him. I'm sorry, but I honestly thought he died years ago," Tom said.
>
> "Well, he didn't forget you. Every time I saw him he'd ask how you were doing. He'd reminisce about the many days you spent over 'his side of the fence' as he put it," mom told him.

"I loved that old house he lived in," Tom said.

"You know Tom, after your father died, Mr Weger stepped in to make sure you had a man's influence in your life."

"He's the one who taught me carpentry," said Tom. "I wouldn't be in this business if it weren't for him. He spent a lot of time teaching me things he thought were important . . . Mom, I'll be there for the funeral," Tom said.

As busy as he was, he kept his word. Tom caught the next flight to his hometown. Mr Weger's funeral was small and uneventful. He had no children of his own, and most of his relatives had passed away.

The night before he had to return home, Tom and his mom stopped last to see the old house next door one more time.

Standing in the doorway, Tom paused for a moment. It was like crossing over into another dimension, a leap through space and time. The house was exactly as he remembered. Every step held memories. Every picture, every piece of furniture . . . Tom stopped suddenly.

"What's wrong, Tom?" his mom asked.

"The box is gone," he said.

"What box?" mom asked.

"There was a small gold box that he kept locked on top of his desk. I must have asked him a thousand times what was inside. All he'd ever tell me it was 'the thing I value most'," Tom said. It was gone.

Everything about the house was exactly how Tom remembered it, except for that box. He figured someone from the Weger family had taken it.

"Now I'll never know what was so valuable to him," Tom said. "I better get some sleep. I have an early flight home, mom."

VALUE-ORIENTED PRIORITIZATION

> It had been about two weeks since Mr Weger died. Returning home from work one day Tom discovered a note in his mailbox. "Signature required on a package. No one at home. Please stop by the main post office within the next three days," the note read.
>
> Early the next day Tom retrieved the package. The small box was old and looked like it had been mailed a hundred years ago. The handwriting was difficult to read, but the return address caught his attention.
>
> "Mr Harold Weger" it read.
>
> Tom took the box out to his car and ripped open the package. There inside was the gold box and an envelope. Tom's hands shook as he read the note inside.
>
> "Upon my death, please forward this box and its contents to Tom Bennett. It's the thing I valued most in my life."
>
> A small key was taped to the letter. His heart racing, and tears filling his eyes, Tom carefully unlocked the box. There inside he found a beautiful gold pocket watch. Running his fingers slowly over the finely etched casing, he unlatched the cover.
>
> Inside he found these words engraved:
>
> "Tom, Thanks for your time! —Harold Weger."
>
> "The thing he valued most . . . was . . . my time."
>
> Tom held the watch for a few minutes, then called his office and cleared his appointments for the next two days.
>
> "Why?" Janice, his assistant asked.
>
> "I need some time to spend with my son," he said.
>
> "Oh, by the way, Janice . . . thanks for your time!"

"Bobby, life is not measured by the number of breaths we take but by the moments that take our breath away. Think about this. You may not realize it, but it's entirely true. At least two people in this world love you so much that they would die for you. At least fifteen people in this world love you in some way. A smile from you can bring happiness to anyone, even if they don't know you."

I looked at Bobby. He didn't need any more words from me; he had already understood what is most important in life!

We reached half an hour late for the game. This would be condemned in the principles of time mastery. But we both knew that this discussion was higher in priority for both of us at the moment when compared with anything else.

9

Time Mastery Techniques

By the time we finished dinner after playing golf, it was almost 9.30 p.m. There was not much time left for anything, and given the physical activity we had for the day, it was time to sleep. Our team relaxed in the lounge after dinner, over a cup of hot tea. For some reason, I remembered *Guinness Book of World Records* that used to come years ago on TV. Towards the end of the programme, the host would say 'We are done for the day, but have just enough time to share this one more world record with you...' and then he would go ahead and share that record.

I took out a booklet from my bag and went over to Bobby. This was a compiled time mastery resource manual* I wanted to give to Bobby. I said, "Bobby, I have a few notes about practical time management strategies that have been collected over years. Always remember, success in life consists of two entities. *Psychology*, which contributes 80 per cent of success and *Strategy*, which accounts for the remaining 20 per cent. We have discussed a lot of psychology, and the notes I am giving you contain the strategy. Go through them, and I promise that they will cut short your journey of 'time mastery'. They essentially include ways people have saved time at the

---
* Included in the book towards the end

workplace, home and even at school or college level. It would make you learn from other people's mistakes, and save you from making your own."

I moved towards my cottage. I looked at the stars; they never seemed to stop amazing me. Unaffected by space or time, they just stood there . . .

10

Beyond Space and Time: Spiritual Approach to Time Mastery

The last day was a rewarding one. It had been almost a week since we had been away from the office and home. The meetings were dedicated to summarizing the major decisions and game plans for the next year. It was time for lunch when the meetings ended. My flight was not until the evening.

It was also the last session with Bobby. Chatting with him had reinstated several time mastery principles for me. I firmly believe that the best way to master an art is to teach it. Teaching embeds the subject matter in one's subconscious mind. Our instructor Joseph during the time mastery seminar had told us that a major reason he did those seminars was to reinstate the principles in his own life. Last week's sessions with Bobby strengthened my conviction on the whole time mastery fundamentals and the transformations it brings in one's life. I remembered the quotation by Mahatma Gandhi, 'The fragrance always remains in the hands that delivers the rose.'

Bobby was ready. He said, "Guru, what's in store for me today?" I was surprised at his addressing me as a 'guru'. I clarified "The role I played with you was of a coach, not a Guru."

I continued, "Just like one needs a coach to learn tennis or football or the guitar, I played the role of a time mastery coach for you during the last week. Our seminar speaker Joseph played a similar role with all the seminar participants. I would rather be known as a time mastery coach who is passionate about improving the quality of people's lives. I know you could coach me on how best to enhance my skills in using Microsoft Excel, where you would become my coach. I guess you wouldn't like to be called a Guru either, would you?"

"Of course not," answered Bobby, and after giving a slight pause added another word to finish his sentence, "Guru." We both smiled.

Today's discussions were not about a lesson and could not be taught. They would come with one's own understanding; one's own experiments with the truth. Still, giving an initiation would help him start his journey in the fourth dimension of 'time mastery'; a dimension that was beyond 'time' and 'space'.

Simply put, the fourth dimension of 'time mastery' was about the 'power of now'; the freedom of thoughts and actions one gets by simply choosing to get excited about life, simply choosing to be truly passionate with a single-minded focus in whatever we do.

This principle is easily seen in the works of excellence. Whenever we confront a true masterpiece, we experience the force of time in a different and more positive way. Perhaps it hits you as you gaze at a classic portrait or a marvel of architectural design. It might strike you as you read a great work of literature or reflect on a classic poem. Perhaps you attend a sporting event and sit mesmerized, watching top athletes perform their magic. The contexts vary but the creative power of time is always there to ponder. How many years did it take? How many hours of practice went into this performance?

The great pyramid of Giza took about 20 years to build. The Taj Mahal required 22 years. The Great Wall of China took centuries to complete. Michelangelo, at the age of 33, spent four years lying on his back to paint the Sistine Chapel. Dante spent 21 years perfecting his *Divine Comedy*. Rod Laver, whom some consider the greatest tennis player of the twentieth century, often practised for six hours *after* a match. Anthony Robbins, world's peak performance coach, has spent over 25 years in perfecting his life-transformation seminar, 'Unleash the Power Within' involving 'fire walk' and three days of continuous performance.

Bobby was toying with his cell phone and diverted my attention. I spoke a little loudly to grab his attention. "Bobby, the obvious question again is, how do you work with, rather than against or in a different direction than, time? The obvious answer is that you must adopt the mentality of a craftsperson. Think of time as an ally, helping you to develop your craft and allowing your product to reach a higher level of maturity and quality. The length of time one invests in an act is an important task as seen in previous examples, but what's most important is a wholehearted, passionate, creative and single-minded dedication towards the task. All 'time masters' have one thing in common: they understand that commitment of being fully present, and when I say present, I mean not just physical, but mental, emotional and spiritual presence at any given moment of time is the supreme requirement to live a life of 'joy' and 'fulfilment'. Being in a perpetual state of some 'other' thought, or being constantly a victim of distractions, such as mindlessly playing with objects while paying attention, would not only reduce the quality of work, but more importantly, reduce the quality of the whole experience. The masters were able to produce their supreme act, because they thoroughly enjoyed the experience of creation; they understood the importance of being present in the 'now.'

"When you appreciate performances of successful movie artists and stage performers, what you are really appreciating is their ability to move you emotionally. This power to move you comes to the artist by being fully present in the moment; by letting themselves be the characters they are playing and not stepping out of it for a split second.

"Being present in the 'now' represents the spiritual approach to time mastery and breaks all bonds and shackles imposed by 'time' itself.

"Living life in the present doesn't mean that we don't plan or apply the time mastery principles we discussed before; it simply means that when we plan, we should do it wholeheartedly with full commitment without letting our thoughts run all over the universe. And we should be passionate about its execution as well.

"Take pride in your experience and be assured that there are no shortcuts on the road to true mastery. Trust that time will bring you to your highest level of mastery. Do your part and have faith in the power of time to do the rest. Realize that even the most gifted need a decade or more of dedicated practice to produce a world-class performance in art, music, science or sports. And you would reach a state when time itself would become unimportant in the journey of time mastery."

The artist in me was turned on and I was giving this speech more as a performer onstage than a friend. The speech was producing the necessary effect on Bobby. It had made him speechless. I knew that he had a lot to digest, and probably a lot more to execute. Time mastery was a humungous subject and would probably take several sessions like these to come close to covering everything, if it was even possible to do so.

But my goal was to cover the most important 20 per cent of the subject that would initiate the 80 per cent results in Bobby, and I felt reasonably confident of achieving the results. Mr Pareto would have been a happy man to know that I had been following and propagating his principles. I decided to share this one last personal experience with Bobby before I left for the airport.

"Bobby," I said with deep emotions coming fresh as I was reminded of the incident I was about to tell.

> It was the year 1986 and I was studying in high school then. I was sitting in the fields with my grandfather. He was unusually excited that day. Growing up as a kid, I had been close to him. I had never seen him in a mood like he was in today. We had been sitting for hours while he was telling me stories. Although I was a grown-up boy now, I still loved his stories. It was almost dark and the time we were to return home. He asked me to stay just a little longer.
>
> Suddenly, I saw an unusual phenomenon occurring in the sky. It was a beautiful ball of light with a long tail, giving it the look of a magician. From my science books, I could guess that it was a comet. I looked at my grandfather with excitement.
>
> He had tears in his eyes. I couldn't understand why he was crying. After a while, he started to speak. "John, almost 76 years ago, when I was a little kid, my grandfather brought me right here at this spot. It was the time when the same comet that appeared now was visible. I didn't know anything about a comet and was shocked to see one. He explained to me that this was the Halley's comet and came only once in 76 years. I had started crying, terrified of seeing something I had never seen before. To stop me from crying, he gave me a watch."

> "From that day onwards, I was waiting for the moment to come again, where I would gift the watch to my grandson on this opportune moment. And today is the moment. John, your presence in my life gives it a new dimension, and today is the moment that defines my life."

"Bobby, there are several moments that define our life. Always be on a lookout for such moments, or for opportunities to create one of them for you and others. And that my friend, is the essence of life."

I took a cab and headed for the airport. I looked at my grandfather's watch all the way. It had stopped working, but the message it gave me was working miracles in my life.

Time Mastery Seminar

Supplement Booklet of Assembled Resources
(Resource Manual)

A – Tactful 'one-liners' to say *no* without hurting others

1. "I can't right now, but I can do it later."
2. "I'm really not the most qualified person for the job."
3. "I just don't have any room in my calendar right now."
4. "I can't, but let me give you the name of someone who can."
5. "I have another commitment."
6. "I'm in the middle of several projects and can't spare the time."
7. "I've had a few things come up and I need to deal with those first."
8. "I would rather decline than end up doing a mediocre job."
9. "I'm really focusing more on my personal and family life right now."
10. "I'm really focusing more on my career right now."
11. "I really don't enjoy that kind of work."

12. "I can't, but I'll be happy to help out with another task."
13. "I've learnt in the past that this really isn't my strong suit."
14. "I'm sure you will do a wonderful job on your own."
15. "I don't have any experience with that, so I can't help you."
16. "I'm not comfortable with that."
17. "I hate to split my attention among too many projects."
18. "I'm committed to leaving some time for myself in my schedule."
19. "I'm not taking on any new projects right now."
20. Or a simple, straight, direct "No" (preferred).

B - Real-life Stories

> I am so busy in my working life, with each week seeming to be more hectic than the previous. There is always so much work going on in those five days at college. The only time I get to spend with family and friends is on the weekends. Plus I have to share the free time between household chores like laundry, cleaning, paying bills and a host of other small things. As a fresher in college, initially I found it very hard to cope. Then I learnt the idea of maintaining a to-do list in which I could write down my tasks. And one by one I could finish them off, be it during the week, or by the weekend. That way I would have a good idea of my tasks and I could prioritize them. In other words, I could take some concrete actions to complete the task. The to-do list is a fascinating and simple method and allows me to remember what I need to do, rather than thinking about what needs to be done and wasting time. This helps me spend more time with my family and close friends. Also, I started paying the bills on time. Of course, over the years I have learnt several other ways to manage time, but I would still recommend beginners in this field to start with at least a to-do list in case you are not already doing so.
>
> **Ajay Ahuja**
Master's Student

> I believe it is human nature to always crave for more time. Sometimes, I feel there isn't enough time in a day to complete a particular task. At other times I have so much time that I wonder how to get over with the day and start with a new one. It's my belief and experience that if we

prioritize our tasks, we might be able to save a lot of time that can be spent with our family and friends. As taught by a dear friend, making a list every week helps. That way I can balance between work and family. I may forget sometimes what I was supposed to do on a particular day of the week or on that certain weekend. However, writing it down in a list assists me to go back to it and make sure the task is done as planned. That's how I and my fiancé work out our schedule as he comes over on the weekends and we have a lot to complete in those two days. But we always make a list of tasks we have to accomplish and finish almost all of them and have some time for ourselves. This way we get to finish the chores and go out for some romantic time together in the evenings.

**Ruchi Goel
Software Engineer**

By nature, I am an extremely lazy person when it comes to mornings. I don't particularly like to go to office. In my previous job, there was no transport arrangement. So my mode of transport was a two-wheeler which gave me the freedom to go and come whenever I wanted every day. Fortunately or unfortunately for me, my manager didn't pay much attention and care about my bad habit either.

However, I've just recently changed jobs. This company is further away from my home, and it has a pick-up and drop facility. For the sheer boredom of travelling in two-wheelers, I decided to use the company car. Who would have thought that something so small would have the most wonderful effect on me? I have started managing my time better since. Now I have no choice but to be ready for pick-up at 9 a.m., if I want to catch the cab. And in the evenings I need to wrap up all my work by 6.30.

In case I ever miss the cab, I know the next one leaves a couple of hours later, so I push in some odd jobs which I wasn't able to do during the day in that time.

V. Sunil Kumar
Software Engineer

I have learnt to be more organized in my work as well as in my personal life. I decide what needs to be done at a specific time and complete the task before moving on to something else. With that I also get to eliminate much unwanted clutter in my life. If there is some important work that requires my full concentration, I wait until after 'office hours' so as not to be interrupted by anyone or anything. That way I can visualize what I want to create in my mind and focus my energies into getting it done.

Communication is an important aspect for me; with myself as well as with my subordinates and superiors. It builds a comfortable level of rapport and a wave of openness for a more coordinated and responsive communication system. A proper communication channel leads to efficient delegation and trust and inspires confidence to get the work done.

You must know your outcome, what you want to achieve by completing a certain task. Your mind must be programmed to finding the quickest method within which to finish off the task. Create a mind map in your head of the outcome as if it already exists. Then specifically define

> to yourself why you want to attain this particular outcome. After that, jot down what specific actions you must undertake in order to achieve your outcome and categorize them. After they have been grouped, simply fit them together in your overall time plan.
>
> **Tonya**
> **Marketing Manager**

> As I grew in ranks in my company, the number of tasks increased proportionally. Initially, I just could not finish every task within the stipulated time frame. Slowly I developed a habit that works beautifully and I still use that habit to manage my time.
>
> Every fortnight I sit down and draw a matrix:
>
> I divide my tasks in four categories:
> a) Long-term (anytime within the next six months)
> b) Mid-term (anytime within the next 2 months)
> c) Short-term (anytime within this month)
> d) Immediate (today or anytime this week)
>
> Also I give a priority to the tasks:
> a) Absolutely needed
> b) Needed
> c) Good if done
>
> Now every day in the morning, I just take a look at the matrix and finish off my jobs one at a time in a more relaxed and methodical manner.
> a) 'Absolutely needed – Immediate' tasks: finish them first.
> b) 'Needed – Immediate' tasks: can be done now or later.

c) 'Absolutely needed – Short-term' tasks.

d) Then depending on the time I have left and the possibility to finish any other task during the day, I keep on doing the tasks.

Sometimes it might happen that I realize that I forgot to add something to the matrix, I immediately do that and see the new matrix.

Basically it is a dynamic process and it is all about maintaining a habit. Once you make it your second nature, everything flows smoothly.

**Ketan Mukadan
Manager, Operations**

I have to thank Rajendra Pawar, 1972 batch IITD, Chairman NIIT and my mentor for many years when I worked in one of his companies, Institute of Quality Limited (IQL).

Whenever I interacted with him, I realized he was extremely good in one aspect. That was to complete transactions on the spot and not to leave them unfinished. In the beginning, it used to surprise me. He would be sitting in the car, heading to office. He would come across something in the paper or in his conversation. He would just pick up the phone and pass on the needed information to the right person on the spot instead of waiting to reach office and hand over the transaction.

As I matured in my role and in my current job as Senior VP, Corporate HR in Bharti Tele-Ventures, one of Asia's fastest growing telecom organizations, I realize the significance of not leaving transactions incomplete and thoroughly eliminating the cycle time for their hand over.

This is also corroborated by the reflections of Philip Crosby, the quality guru who says the quality of life is all about completed transactions and successful relationships.

Unfinished or WIP transactions that we hold and postpone to tomorrow are amongst the worst stress-creators. Technology is a big aid today in helping relieve that stress by quickly directing the transaction to the appropriate action person or closing it on the spot. I have a cell phone and a blackberry that help me to do precisely that. Of course, the starting point is a mindset of not postponing. Without that, no technology or other aid will help.

So, even though I have a fairly diverse set of responsibilities in my existing job, this is one of the critical success factors in helping me manage my role without an undue build-up of stress.

Of course I need to ask my team members and colleagues if my ability to quickly pass on or deal with transactions becomes stressful for them. But that should be material for another story I guess.

Vinit Taneja
Sr. Vice President, Corporate Human Resources,
Bharti Telecom

C – Time Mastery Techniques at the Workplace (That Work!)*

Time mastery techniques can be divided in two categories – *mechanical* or *behavioural* techniques. Mechanical techniques are those that can be put into practice immediately without the necessity of a behavioural change. In other words, you don't have to form a new habit in order to make them work for you. For example, changing the location of your telephone from your desk to the wall behind you (in case you have one) is a mechanical idea. When the phone rings you have to turn around to pick it up, which means you will be facing the wall, with your back to the doorway. Since you will avoid eye contact, most people will not try to talk to you while you are on the phone. This idea will work immediately, because you don't have to form the habit of turning around – you *have* to turn around in order to pick up the phone.

Behavioural techniques are those that require a behavioural change in order to make them work. You have to form a new habit. This could take weeks of persistence. Generally as a thumb rule, a habit practised for three weeks has an excellent chance of becoming a permanent part of your life.

For example, if you are currently in the habit of talking on the phone without making notes, a behavioural idea that could save time would be to start recording all calls in a systematic way. This ensures that nothing is forgotten, reduces follow-up calls, and increases concentration and so on. But you have to form the new habit before you can reap the rewards of the idea.

Note that you could practise several mechanical techniques to help you form a behaviour. For example, you could ensure buying a phone system with an inbuilt notepad system and a fixed pen that would constantly remind you of making notes.

---

* Inputs from Harold Taylor's website www.taylorintime.com

Mechanical techniques are plentiful, and since they require no behaviour change, any number of them could be put into practice simultaneously. Although the time saved by each idea may be minimal, collectively they add up to hours. Behavioural techniques, on the other hand, would be overwhelming if you introduced more than one or two at a time. They take several weeks before they become habitual. But the payback, in terms of time saved, is usually much greater than the same number of mechanical techniques.

Here is a list of 100 behavioural (with a few mechanical ones) techniques that could serve as a checklist for you! Make sure to think of mechanical techniques pertaining to your own environment that would help you reinstate the behaviour.

Techniques:

1. Hire the right people to perform the tasks. Human resource forms the backbone of any organization.
2. Assemble the team first before starting a task.
3. Do rigorous timeline-driven project management.
4. Put your personal and organizational goals in writing.
5. Every week do something that brings you closer to your annual goals.
6. Schedule *appointments with yourself* to complete priority work.
7. Schedule more time for tasks than you think it will take.
8. Set priorities according to importance, not urgency.
9. Make notes while you are talking on the telephone.
10. Use a *Delegation Record* or *Assignment Record* to keep track of assignments to others.
11. Develop the *do-it-now* habit. Don't delay.
12. Have meetings start on time, end on time and have a timed agenda.

13. Take advantage of commuting time, travel time and waiting time to get things done.
14. Toss out as much correspondence and paperwork as possible.
15. Don't write a letter when a telephone call will do.
16. Don't call when an email will do.
17. Make minor decisions quickly.
18. Set deadlines on all tasks you delegate.
19. Be time-conscious rather than a perfectionist. Let the amount of time spent on a task be proportionate to the value of the outcome.
20. Hold meetings only when absolutely necessary, and *keep them brief.*
21. Keep telephone conversations brief; discuss the business upfront.
22. Write brief letters, reports and e-mail. Encourage brevity in others.
23. When a crisis occurs, immediately determine how to stop a recurrence.
24. Say "no" more often. Have as much respect for your own time as you have for other people's time.
25. Say "no" to the project, not the person. You cannot do everything everyone asks you to do.
26. Use a *Participant's Action Sheet* at meetings to record notes.
27. Take advantage of time-saving technology such as handheld computers, business card scanners and remote access software.
28. Don't allow upward delegation. Ask for solutions, not problems.
29. Start earlier in the morning if possible. Utilize your *prime time* for priorities.
30. Don't keep magazines. Tear out or photocopy relevant articles.

31. Plan as far in advance as feasible.
32. Record the whole year's schedule of meetings and events into your planner.
33. Always carry a small scratch pad, pocket recorder or handheld computer to record notes and capture ideas.
34. Use the same planner for home and office. Schedule time for family events as well as work.
35. Be in control of your own life; don't let others' lack of planning become your crisis.
36. Have set times (not more than two specific times unless you are in internet business) each day to review your e-mail. Assign a time limit.
37. Always take a few minutes after each meeting to evaluate how it went.
38. If someone calls for an appointment, try to settle the matter right there on the telephone.
39. When leaving a message for someone to call you back, indicate a convenient time to call.
40. If the person you are calling is not in, try to get the information you need from someone else.
41. Record the time you must leave the office when travelling to a distant meeting.
42. If items dropped in your in-basket distract you, move the basket from your desk.
43. When away on a business trip, have someone else sort and dispense with most of your mail.
44. To reduce interruptions during the day, hold brief stand-up meetings with your staff each morning.
45. When filing paperwork, record a *throw out* date on it to make subsequent purging easier.
46. Schedule specific amounts of time to review and dispense with your mail and voice mail.

47. Hold brief breakfast meetings when most people are mentally alert and have a full day to take action.
48. Capture ideas when listening to cassette tapes or CDs by dictating into a pocket recorder.
49. Use checklists for recurring events such as meetings, sales calls and business trips.
50. Spend time each week on *time investments* – those activities that will help you free up more time.
51. When putting something in your follow-up file, make a corresponding note in your planner that tells you it is there.
52. Recognize you cannot do everything. Work on the 20 per cent of the activities that produce 80 per cent of your results.
53. Tackle tough jobs first – quit doing petty tasks and tackle the big jobs first. Remember the 80/20 rule. You will find that you will be able to finish big jobs without stress.
54. Manage stress by putting life in perspective, and not taking yourself too seriously.
55. Clarify goals and resources for every task.
56. Before assigning a task to someone, make sure that the person feels that he owns the job. Instil ownership in each member by developing a shared vision. Selection of this one key person ensures success.
57. List every task and break down the task to minuscule steps.
58. Determine the limiting step of every task and brainstorm on the actions that would make it possible.
59. Organize the tasks into two categories – sequential and parallel. Sequential tasks need a prerequisite to be completed whereas parallel tasks can be done simultaneously.
60. Plan month-wise, week-wise, day-wise, hour-wise.

61. Understand your unique talents. What have you done excellent in the past? What do you do well? What are your key results areas?
62. Concentrate on doing only the one or two of the tasks that utilize your unique talent.
63. Define your customer in each and every task. Repeatedly ask, 'How do I please my customer?' Customer can be your boss, manager, client or user of the end product your company develops.
64. Take time to understand why are you on a payroll. What is the result or product you are expected to generate?
65. Delegate and develop others – delegation is not a dumping ceremony. Break the "Do-It-Yourself" habit and let others learn to share responsibility in operating the business. You will find you have more time for major tasks.
66. Delegation of job is a helpful tool; only if you understand that you still own the outcome and you may have to stay on top of things.
67. Learn how to delegate effectively. This means picking the right person, giving clear directions, setting benchmark and due dates, and then letting them do it.
68. Read a paper or e-mail and address an issue a maximum of one time.
69. Use the TRAF policy - Toss, Refer/Delegate, Action, File (Use option file sparingly as you would have to refer to the document again).
70. Use a follow-up file to hold paperwork relating to scheduled tasks.
71. If a new task comes and is added to your W5H?/To Do list, write it before performing it.
72. Organize the W5H?/To Do lists. Separate the 'urgent' from 'important'. Separate the 'important' from 'not important'.

73. Your W5H? list should serve as a blueprint. Take action according to this blueprint only.
74. Distinguish between 'creative procrastination' and 'general procrastination'. Some tasks can be creatively procrastinated till a point where you may never have to do them without having any negative effect. Use the tool of 'creative procrastination' for saving time.
75. Set your own deadlines. Setting deadlines and telling others becomes an ego fight and you go to extremes to get it done.
76. Buy a week-at-a-glance appointment book and use it religiously. Write everything that you need to accomplish in this book. This book is your brain!
77. Distinguish between the urgent and the vital. The urgent may be making much noise to get your attention, but it is rarely vital that it be done right now or at all.
78. "The vital task rarely needs to be done today. The urgent task calls for instant action. The momentary appeal of these tasks seems irresistible, and they devour our energy. With a sense of loss we recall the vital tasks we pushed aside. We realize that we have become slaves to the tyranny of the urgent." —Charles Hummel
79. The key is not to prioritize what is on your schedule, but to schedule your priorities.
80. Keep track of your time by 15-minute increments for two weeks to see how you actually spend your time. Compare this to what you should be or want to be spending your time on. It will give you the motivation to make the needed changes.
81. Procrastination has many different causes: fear, boredom, perfectionism, an overwhelming task and unclear goals. Identify the reason behind procrastination, so you are solving the right problem when dealing with it.

82. If you earn $10,000 a year, each minute is worth $.09. If you earn $30,000 a year, each minute is worth. $.26. Use these thoughts to help you prioritize your activities and to determine to whom you should be delegating. Any time you are doing work that someone at a lower wage could be doing, you are losing money.
83. Set goals. They help you prioritize your activities and you know that you have succeeded.
84. There are 1,440 minutes in a day and 29020 days in an 80-year lifetime. Take control of your time and make this year the year you do what you want.
85. Consolidate similar tasks/group similar jobs and do them concurrently. This eliminates a lot of sporadic behaviour.
86. Learn to use idle time – when there seems to be down time, read a book, write a memo or plan what needs to be done in the business.
87. Avoid the cluttered desk syndrome – a clear desk helps you to think clearly, locate papers easier and keep your mind on the task at hand.
88. Get started immediately on important tasks – no matter how much you hate doing a task, do it. Remember, you must change old habits.
89. Try rewarding yourself at the end of the day. This will motivate self-discipline.
90. Reduce meeting time – ask yourself if a meeting is necessary. Will a phone call do just as well? If a meeting is a must, try a stand-up one; this will guarantee that the important issue is addressed. Take time to plan – without it, how will you know what needs to be accomplished for a day, week, month or several years?
91. Identify "best time" for work: Everyone has high and low periods of attention and concentration. Are you a "morning person" or a "night person"? Use your power

times to study and work; use the down times for routines such as shopping and errands.
92. Do difficult work first: When you are fresh, you can process information more quickly and save time as a result.
93. While studying, use distributed learning and practice: study in shorter time blocks with short breaks between. This keeps you from getting fatigued and 'wasting time'. This type of studying is efficient because while you are taking a break, the brain is still processing the information.
94. Make sure the surroundings are conducive to work: This will allow you to reduce distractions that can 'waste time'.
95. Make room for entertainment and relaxation. Life is more than work and study. You need to have a social life; you need to have a balance in your life.
96. Make sure you have time to sleep and eat properly: sleep is often an activity (or lack of activity) that people use as their time management 'bank'.
97. Try to combine activities. Use the 'twofer' concept. If you are travelling in a bus, carry your psychology notes to study. If you are waiting in line for tickets to the Stings concert, bring your biology flashcards to memorize.
98. Avoid marathon study or work sessions. Schedule two-hour sessions. Take a 10-minute break every hour.
99. Set specific goals for each session.
100. Remember the lines, 'If you can't be a pine at the top of a hill, be a scrub in the valley, but be the best scrub wherever you are . . .'

Starting Off: Action Sheet

In order to get started, choose three ideas that make sense to you, and that you would be willing to start practising. Record them on the following Action Sheet, select a starting date, and go to it! Remember to persist for three weeks to allow time for a habit to develop if the ideas are *behavioural* in nature. Once they are working successfully, choose three more and work on those.

Three of the most useful ideas:
1.
2.
3.

Since small successes are motivational, I will ask you to start with a series of simple mechanical steps. Clean up your work area, get rid of superfluous material, move your in basket off your desk, make up a follow-up file, arrange your materials so they are close at hand. Then choose a behavioural idea that would eliminate a time-waster that you are experiencing. For example, if papers tend to accumulate on your desk and you waste time shuffling papers, build the habit of scheduling paperwork in the follow-up file for later action. If you are for ever interrupting yourself and others as questions pop into your mind, start using a *Delegation Record* or *Communications Record* to accumulate those questions. If you are putting off important tasks because you don't have time, break the tasks into smaller chunks and schedule them in your planner to work on at specific times. Each time a behavioural idea has been fully mastered, pick another one and work on it until it too has been incorporated into your daily routine.